INTRODUCTION TO DATA ARCHITECTURE

A FOUNDATION COVERING BASIC CONCEPTS OF THEORY AND PRACTICE

JOHN PARKINSON

The UK Copyright Service

Permissions

A significant amount of time was spent in investigation of permissions necessary for the quotations of speech and text that appear in this book. Unfortunately much guidance available is self-contradictory. As a result, whilst not having any association with Wiley-Blackwell, I have used the permissions guidelines provided to Wiley-Blackwell authors (available online as a reference) as a guideline for this book. This guidance document is clear, concise, and unambiguous, and references the Publisher's Association guidelines. Where I have quoted larger portions of text, or images clearly subject to copyright, these permissions are noted below or at the relevant point in the text.

Throughout this book, I refer to the Data Management Body of Knowledge (*Data Management Body of Knowledge*, DAMA-BOK, Mosely et Al, Data Management Association, 2010). As explained in the relevant chapter, there are a number of best practice data management frameworks already in existence and I had no wish to create another. This naturally meant that I needed to choose a framework already in existence. I have chosen the DAMA framework, as I personally believe it is simple, clear and comprehensive. As a result numerous quotations from the *Data Management Body of Knowledge* exist in this book, and all are appropriately attributed. The shorthand of DAMA-BOK is also used as opposed to "DAMA Data Management Body of Knowledge." Note that the DAMA Body of Knowledge states:

I also gratefully acknowledge the permission from Technics publications to use material from *Data Modeling Made Simple: A Practical Guide for Business and IT Professionals.*

I gratefully acknowledge The Open Group for permission to incorporate figure 5-1 of its copyrighted material from TOGAF Version 9.1. TOGAF and The Open Group are registered trademarks of The Open Group.

Dedication

This book is dedicated to all the people who have encouraged me to continue writing

You know who you are.

Acknowledgments

One does not complete a book like this entirely by oneself. In this case, I would like to thank the following:

Editor:
Jenny Bowskill

Exterior Design:
Author

Typesetting and Interior Design:
Author

Most importantly, I need to thank my long-suffering wife Kirsty who has had me spouting data (in all its forms) at her for years.

John Parkinson, 2023

About the Author

Every day organisations across the globe capture, collate, transform, present and utilise information. Information flows within an organisation from a contact centre through a myriad of information stores towards financial planning and reporting and finally to the executive and potentially a regulator. However, large organisations are typically fragmented, and whilst information specialists exist within islands at each stage, communication failures between these islands are the pain points in information quality today. In many organisations, business and information technology professionals sometimes appear incapable of connecting.

Twenty years ago the same applied to architects and civil engineers. One forward-thinking institution ran a "Civil Engineering and Architecture" degree cramming an architecture degree and a civil engineering degree together, with the aim of creating individuals who could talk across both professions. This was my degree. It was a good grounding, as it taught how to reconcile individuals with different agendas and bring both parties together on a journey. In those days the journey was to create a great building. Now my journey is bringing business and IT professionals together to create data quality.

In the last years of the last century the building industry (and the rest of the economy) entered a recession and I changed career to study as an accountant. Three years later a Chartered Accountant started wondering where the information on which my profession relied came from. I then started worrying, wondering, reading, and learning about data.

My company was heavily involved in mergers of building societies, and I spent time working as a consultant scrutineer for the UK regulator. These large data quality engagements involved hundreds of people working to remediate data to meet regulatory expectations and legal requirements.

On the way I learned:
- About project management and how it can be an interesting challenge and a thankless task.
- About data quality and how bad it usually is.
- About data remediation and the problems it faces.
- About data transformation and migration and common problems.

- About data analysis & profiling and how useful it can be.
- About business process, its effect on data, and its transformation and migration and what a difference it can make.
- About data governance (and lack of) and how important that is.
- Many broader skills like stakeholder management.
- A fair bit about technology.

I also worked with many clients across many sectors on data and business process related engagements. This work covered data strategy, data governance and data quality, data and process analysis and design, financial and data modelling as well as finance and risk transformation. Over time I turned into a professional with wide experience and knowledge in the field.

I am still a Chartered Accountant; however over time have also become a PRINCE2 Practitioner, a TOGAF 9.1 Enterprise Architect, and a Certified Information Systems Auditor (CISA). I have first-hand experience of a wide range of technology products across information design, management, discovery and governance and have certifications in both Google and Amazon cloud services.

At the time of writing I hold the position of Chief Data Architect for a major international bank. I have also had the honour of being invited to speak at a number of conferences on the subject of data architecture, data governance and data quality. I regularly write articles for publication worldwide.

I am a member of ICAEW (Institute of Chartered Accountants), ISACA (Information Systems and Control Association), AEA (Association of Enterprise Architects), The International Association for Information and Data Quality (IAIDQ), and the Data Management Association (DAMA).

In my spare time I am a keen rock climber and runner. I hope you enjoy reading this book as much as I have enjoyed writing it.

John Parkinson, 2023

About the Reader

A far more important consideration than any information about the author is about you, the reader. Who is the author writing this book for, and why? This consideration is critical, as in order to pitch a book at a consistent level, one has to make assumptions about a reader's level of knowledge.

I think the best description would be that it is aimed at a younger me – specifically a me who was attending a meeting about his career, and was fascinated with data, data flow, data in organisations, and told an older and wiser individual this was the case. The older, wiser individual said "it sounds like you are talking about enterprise data architecture." I'd never heard of this at the time.

Many years later, I ended up as Chief Enterprise Data Architect for a multinational bank. Along the way I discovered that there are as many definitions of a data architect as there are people working in IT, and I really wish someone had written a book covering the basics that would have saved me a vast amount of time in misunderstanding, wrong turns, and wasted effort.

I can't go back and give this book to a younger me, but I'm sure there are many others out there in the same position but different points in their career. I hope this book will be useful to them.

So what are my assumptions?

I have assumed the reader wants to know more about data architecture. Since they have bought a book entitled "Introduction to Data Architecture" I'm assuming that they are at the shallow end of knowledge, and not an expert looking to pick holes.

I would note here that I have simplified many areas and given a high level explanation. Sometimes a high level explanation does not tell the full story, but for the necessity of space conservation it needs to be the one used.

In an attempt to make the book as relevant to as many people as possible, I have started with an overview and then delved further into detail as the book progresses. It follows that some sections of the book are therefore more aimed at the high level and other sections at those who are more focused on the detail.

- For the newcomer to data architecture – the person like the younger me, I hope you will read the entire book.
- For the CIOs (Chief Information Officers) you are likely to be most interested in the first section, to understand the value that data architecture brings you. I hope you will be open to employing data architects as a regular part of your workforce.
- For the CDOs (Chief Data Officers), I hope this book can help you understand who you work with, who are your partners in data and how we can help each other.
- For Project Managers, I hope this books helps you understand why you need data architects on your projects.
- For Solution Architects, I hope this book helps you understand who you can go to for the data specialism.
- For Developers, the same. So you can know what data architects do, and where they fit in to the process of creating solutions, what our specialism is, and how we can help you.

Summary: A Foundation

I have tried to make this book useful to all readers who wish to understand more about Data Architecture. I've tried to cover the basics of both theory and practice, and also give insight into what Data Architecture involves as a day to day role if you are looking to make Data Architecture your career.

I have also covered (again at a high level) what a data architect needs to know. What are the building blocks of information flow, and how do they link together. I have covered best practice, but also common pain points with real-life organisational data architecture, and the solutions that may be employed.

That said, this book does not cover every system that may exist in every organisation. But its intention is to share the knowledge that accelerates data architecture understanding and facilitates accumulation of knowledge when working in the real world.

Table of Contents

SECTION 1: What is Data Architecture?

SECTION 2: Building Blocks

SECTION 3: Implementation

SECTION 1: What is Data Architecture?

- Book Introduction.

- What is Data Architecture?

- The types of Data Architecture.

- What does a Data Architect do? How does this differ between a Project Data Architect and an Enterprise Data Architect?

- How do we govern Data Architecture?

Chapter 1: Book Introduction

Where to start? I would like to introduce the book, why I decided to write this book, and describe its structure. This not only gives a sense of the "story" I wish to tell, but also allows the reader to understand which part of the book may contain the information they seek.

Why Did I Write This Book?

Some time ago, I used to write articles on a weekly basis and publish them on my blog. These articles covered the whole spectrum of data, specifically data architecture, data quality, data strategy, data governance and data management. I tried to write about subjects within data that I found interesting, but also areas where I felt that knowledge was lacking, and that some explanation would help data and non-data professionals understand each other a bit better.

Reactions to these articles varied. Given the measure-everything nature of the Internet, I was able to track how many people read the articles I wrote, how many times they were shared, how many times they were "liked" – all the usual functionality. I trickled along happily writing articles, generally flying under the radar – though some articles were picked up by magazines and reprinted with my permission. Most of the articles were dealing with a subset of data, not a broad brush question such as "What is Data Architecture?" so, one week I thought I'd tackle that particular subject.

The response was amazing. This single article generated almost a hundred times more interest than anything else I had written. I was blown away.

This got me thinking. I was at that point in the depths of the sequel to "The Data Quality Blueprint" – a book that will eventually become "The Data Governance Blueprint." However, like my first book, it is huge – a one stop shop for everything about data governance. I'd completed the text, and had hundreds of diagrams to put together. It was going slow.

I thought that putting together a relatively high level book covering the basics of data architecture would be useful to many – certainly on the basis of the interest generated in the article. What's more, I already had a lot of pre-existing material that could be used. Yes they would need reformatting, but surely this would be a relatively easy write?

Appearances can be deceptive! More or less everything has been rewritten. However the basic intent remains – to provide a high level overview of Data Architecture.

Important Note

This book is designed to be both realistic and, more than anything else, *practical*. As such, the vast majority of the book covers the practice of data architecture as it exists now (2023).

Many data architecture books concentrate on the bleeding-edge, the brand-new data constructs just-into-the-market. Whilst this book does cover these systems, the *reality* is that most data in most organisations is contained in older systems.

This book covers both system designs decades old - which a practicing data architect *will* see and *will* have to deal with all the time - and the shiny and new, which frankly may only be encountered occasionally.

In short, this is a holistic book covering all types of systems that may turn up after you walk into an organisation. Because that's what a practicing Data Architect needs to know about. Its not just the new stuff, or just the old stuff.

Construction of The Book

The book is divided into three roughly equal sections:

Section 1: What is Data Architecture?

This first section answers the question "What is Data Architecture?" It takes the reader through Data Architecture (the plumbing), Data Architecture (the discipline) and Data Architecture (the role).

By the end of this section the reader should understand what Data Architecture is, and be able to accurately describe what a Data Architect would be doing on a day-to-day basis, and how they bring value to the organisation.

Section 2: Building Blocks.

The second section takes the reader through the various components of data architecture that exist in IT systems today. What are the building blocks that comprise our information ecosystems? What do they do, how do they link together, and why should you choose one variety over another?

Section 3: Implementation

The third section brings all this together. It connects the building blocks into architectural solutions, examines real life pain points and covers how they can be solved.

Chapter 2: What is Data Architecture?

So, let us start with the basics – What is Data Architecture?

Exciting, isn't it?

The first thing to mention is that Data Architecture is exciting. Information weaves and flows around the organisation. It ducks and dives, it merges and splits, some stays where it's put and some never stays still, some is set in stone, and some changes all the time. And all the time, every second of every day, people and machines use information to make decisions. Big decisions about investing and divesting in mega-corporations, or smaller decisions about whether to give a customer a loan.

To manage all this is the province, the life, the reason for existence, of the Data Architect. Taming and controlling information flow so that the right information gets to the right people at the right time. What a great job.

Joe Mckendrick at dbta.com said it well:

"the design and creation of modern data architectures is an uplifting process that brings in the whole enterprise, stimulating new ways of thinking, collaborating, and planning for data and information requirements. It's an opportunity for business decision makers to sit down with IT colleagues and figure out what kind of business they want to be in, what kinds of information they seek to propel that business forward, and what needs to be done to capture and harness that information."

I wouldn't disagree with any of that.

Starting at the Basics

Unfortunately, like Governance, Quality and Strategy, there's a lot of misconceptions about Data Architecture.

In the world of Wikipedia, we have a statement on the lines of:

"data architecture is composed of models, policies, rules or standards that govern which data is collected, and how it is stored, arranged, integrated, and put to use in data systems and in organizations."

This doesn't really sound fun. It sounds dry as dust. Also, it's not quite right. It describes some of the tools used by Data Architecture "the discipline" rather than Data Architecture "the plumbing."

So let's start by splitting things up:

- Data Architecture (the plumbing) is the way in which information flows around the organisation. What is plumbed from where to where.
- Data Architecture (the discipline) is the effort to control it. The design, the models, policies, rules, standards. Anything that designs the pipework and tries to get the contents (the data) to the right place at the right time.
- The Data Architect being the person who does one to try and control the other.

The word "architecture" doesn't help either. People get confused about the word "architecture." It has an inherent mental mapping to bricks and mortar, and struggles to translate to the world of technology. So it helps if we can replace the word "architecture" with "design."

More confusion now starts to creep in – even amongst the tech-savvy – as "designing the data" is a bit abstract. Design what? The answer is Information and Information Flow. I will cover this in great depth later, - in fact, in a way, the vast majority of the book answers this question. But first, I will cover some misconceptions.

What are the Misconceptions?

So, getting a little serious for a second, what are the misconceptions that plague Data Architecture?

- The first misconception is that Data Architects are pure technologists. This is not true. Data Architects (in my view) need to understand the business need for information and how it should be delivered. They must understand the business requirement to make decisions, and how those decisions are based on information. It is the Data Architect's job to get that information to the right place at the right time so the right decisions can be made. Data Architects – like Enterprise Architects – need to bridge the business/technology divide. Data bridges the divide, so the architects have to as well.

- The second misconception is that Data Architects are "just" data modellers, database administrators, or database designers. I would disagree. Whilst data models and databases are included in the wider description of Data Architecture (the plumbing), Data Architecture is both wider and shallower than both data modelling or database administration. Equating the roles not only does a disservice to the horizon-to-horizon view of the architects, but also to the exceptional detailed knowledge of the modellers and database admins.

- The third misconception is that we don't need data architects. That actually "solution architects do the job anyway." This is the (unfortunately not-uncommon) IT-centric view, which views the hardware and software as the important bits and the data as the parcel that is passed around. This view has done nothing good for information in the last thirty years. In reality it is the data which is the important (and fun) bit and the hardware and software need to play nicely. Actually my personal view is slightly more nuanced in that we don't need solution-level data architects on smaller projects as long as there is a central architecture function (i.e. the enterprise data architect) engaged, and/or the solution architects are data-savvy. On larger projects, however, a Data Architect is a must.

How Does This Work in Practice?

So after these misconceptions, where is the truth? Let us take the example of the data in a typical organisation. It is, unfortunately, a sad and unhappy tale. In some cases a tragedy, in some cases a horror story.

It's probably a mess. There is some form of core system that is proprietary or historical. It's pretty much stable as long as you don't try to change it. It's also absolutely critical, and plumbed into everything else. The problem is that it doesn't really do what the organisation needs.

A historical system may have been brilliant once, but the world has moved on, different products are sold, different information is needed, and the business model has changed. A proprietary system was probably never a perfect fit for the organisation in the first place, but the vendor promised that it would solve the world's problems. This turned out to not be entirely true.

Many years later, the overall data flow in the organisation will be a conglomerate of:

- bolt-ons
- work arounds
- tactical solutions
- mashups
- and sticking plasters
- ....which enable the whole ensemble to (roughly) function.

Data flow, in this hypothetical organisation, doesn't get to the right people at the right time for them to make the right decisions. In fact, data is often of poor quality, not complete, not accurate, not timely and generally doesn't meet business needs. As a result the organisation wastes money, time and resources, loses profitability and discards shareholder value.

The role of the Data Architect is to take this sorry story and transform it into a bestseller. To put it succinctly, to control design and flow of data.

As a result the Data Architect will, at an enterprise level (often called "Enterprise Data Architects"):

- Define the data vision by interpreting the business vision.
- Define how the business information requirements will be met.
- Work with the business to define requirements.
- Translate these to tech language so the pure technologists can create something great.
- Understand the data strategy and – importantly – have a good idea of how to implement it.

- Define data standards, and principles. These may be modelling standards, metadata standards, security standards, reference data standards, and many others.
- Define a reference architecture (a pattern that others can follow).
- Define how data should flow within the organisation.

At a project level they will:

- Work with projects and project management to create understanding about the importance of data flow.
- Work with solution architects to ensure that the proposed solution aligns with the overall strategy of the organisation.
- Work with solution architects to ensure that the proposed solution meets current and future business requirements.
- Understand and guide the way in which the solution links with the overall information flows within the organisation.
- Put projects in touch with other projects which are trying to do the same thing to similar data.
- Try and limit tactical solutions for data. It is remarkably easy for data to get out of hand very quickly.

Summary

In short, anything that affects the flow of information around the organisation will (or should) fall under the remit of the Data Architect.

They are the people who take the vast corporate information factory and steer it in the direction the business wants and the organisation needs.

Exciting, isn't it?

Chapter 3: Data Disciplines Explained

Introduction

The next area I will cover is the relationship between data architecture and other data disciplines, specifically;

- Data Governance
- Data Management.
- Data Quality
- Data Strategy

This allows the reader to place data architecture in its context, and also to understand what is covered - and not covered - by the role. The answer to this question is confused by the way the disciplines exist in organisations. In many cases there is no clear standard of responsibility across the organisation. In fact this confusion applies both within and without the data world.

In this chapter I will set out my own view on how the disciplines interact. I strongly believe that there is clear demarcation between them, however also that they all need to work together to succeed.

I would stress that this chapter is at a high level and cannot cover every nuance of complex subject matter. Data is a moving, living and continuously evolving organism and if I delved deep then this chapter would be the longest in the book.

Throughout this chapter, I will use the processes in a restaurant as an analogy to aid understanding and help clarify the picture. The menu, so to speak, is Quality > Governance > Strategy > Management > Architecture.

Data Quality

> *Quality is never an accident. It is always the result of intelligent effort.*
>
> John Rushkin

Any organisational process can be considered as a series of linked decisions. Each of those decisions requires information. This applies whether the decision is a board decision for an acquisition – in which case the information will include strategic benefit and profitability, or a decision to lend money – in which case the information will include customer earning power and existing commitments.

Decisions are based on data – therefore data underpins everything any organisation does. As a result, poor data is primarily not an IT problem but a business problem. However it is not unusual for the word "data" to result in a turn-off to business engagement. In reality IT may own the pipes by which data is transmitted, but the business owns the data. If the data is wrong it will be the business taking poor decisions which will create a negative business impact.

However data, as stated above, is not static. Information flows within an organisation from a contact centre through a myriad of information stores towards financial planning and reporting and finally to the executive and potentially a regulator. Data therefore must arrive at the right place. It must also arrive at the right time. There is no point in the right data being delivered late.

Data Quality is what we are trying to achieve. The right data, at the right place, at the right time, to the right people in order that they can make the right decisions. Data Quality is our aim.

To use our analogy of a restaurant, and if our decision maker is the customer, to whom the data is served, data quality is the great experience of the taste-surpassing dish, matching their order, cooked to perfection and served on a spotless plate, at the perfect time after they sit down.

Right Data + Right Place + Right Time = Quality.

Data Governance

Data Governance is often misunderstood. Some consider "Data Governance" to be simply allocating individuals as data owners and stewards, together with the creation of a data dictionary and a data model. In reality the span of Data Governance is far wider, and far more complex.

Data Governance is an integral component of corporate governance. It acts to set direction for data management, and thence to align data management with the risk appetite of the organisation. This view is echoed by industry standards.

The DAMA (Data Management Association) body of knowledge (DM-BOK) defines data governance as follows:

"The exercise of authority, and control (planning, monitoring and enforcement) over the management of data assets"

Similarly, ISACA's COBIT Framework states:

"Information governance ensures that:

Stakeholder needs, conditions and options are evaluated to determine balanced, agreed-on enterprise objectives, which are to be achieved through the acquisition and management of information resources.

Direction is set for information management capabilities through prioritisation and decision making.

Performance and compliance of the information resource are monitored against agreed-on direction and objectives."

This is all very well, but what does it actually mean in terms of day to day actions? Here I will again quote the DAMA framework, which splits Data Governance into "Data Management Planning" and "Data Management Control", the components of each being shown below.

Data Management Planning:

- Understand strategic enterprise data needs.
- Develop and maintain the data strategy.
- Establish data professional roles and organisations.
- Identify and appoint data stewards.
- Establish Data Governance and stewardship organisations.
- Develop and approve data polices, standards and procedures.
- Review and approve data architecture.
- Plan and sponsor data management projects and services.
- Estimate data asset value and associated costs.

Data Management Control:

- Supervise data professional organisations and staff.
- Co-ordinate data management activities.
- Manage and resolve data related issues.
- Monitor and ensure regulatory compliance.
- Monitor and ensure conformance with data standards, policies and architecture.
- Oversee data management projects and services.
- Communicate and promote the value of data assets.

We need to emphasise here that with a few exceptions where Data Governance has the responsibility for creation, the data strategy being one, data governance mostly acts to ensure that others do their job to the required standard, and to create a framework – people and process – to facilitate this.

To continue my restaurant analogy "food" governance will, amongst other things;

- Come up with the strategy of how the restaurant should quality assure its food.
- Plan how relevant legislation (food standards and hygiene) will be met.
- Approve and monitor quality control initiatives.

...and generally have a watching brief on everything in the restaurant to make sure things go right and the customer gets their taste sensation.

Data Strategy

> *"Information should ultimately support the goal of any enterprise — deliver value for its stakeholders — which translates to enterprise goals that should be achieved"*
>
> COBIT 5, Enabling Information, ISACA

The Data Strategy – which is a product of data governance – describes the long term aim for data in the organisation. It is derived from the corporate strategy and the corporate vision, and sets out how the organisation will achieve information needs over the longer term.

As each data strategy is different there is no holistic template, however components of a data strategy would commonly include:

- Scope
- Purpose of the Strategy
- Information Needs of the Organisation
- Key Information Principles
- Information Governance
- Information Management
- Information Policy and Practice
- Information Management Lifecycle
- Information Architecture
- Knowledge Sharing and Collaboration
- Learning and Development

In short, the data strategy is "what we need to achieve and how we are going to get there" – albeit at a high level.

In our restaurant, the data strategy is the analysis of diner preferences, an estimate of demand in the local area, the number of waiters needed and how big a restaurant is required. It includes how we are going to train waiters and chefs, and not least, what we will put in place to ensure that the quality dish gets to the customer to create that great experience we talked about earlier.

Data Management

So, if Data Governance is the overall watching brief and high level strategy, what is Data Management?

Data Management is simply the day to day operation to manage data. I'm going to use the DAMA framework again, not least for consistency, but also because it contains a laudably clear description of the activities that sit within Data Management. These are:

- Data Architecture Management.
- Data Operations Management (which includes, amongst other elements, creation of data models).
- Data Development.
- Data Security Management.
- Metadata Management.
- Data Quality Management.
- Reference and Master Data Management.
- Document and Content Management.

It cannot be stressed too much that these are the *day-to-day* operations. "Data Quality Management" does not equal data quality, but is the day to day function of reporting on data quality, feeding back exceptions to business teams, developing data quality procedures, and evaluating data quality service levels. Of course it acts to further our progress towards the goal, but does not equal the goal. The difference is important.

Going back to my hypothetical restaurant, data management is all the operations to ensure things go right. Checking the freezer and the oven temperatures are as required, checking freshness of ingredients, checking pans to ensure they are clean and checking of the order before its cooked so the right dish is created, and ensuring that tonight we've got the right number of waiters for the anticipated demand.

I will note here that I am not covering the creation of the ingredients – or, back in the data world, the business processes that create the data. In the same way that no food will taste nice if the ingredients are out of date, no data discipline will ever be able to compensate for poor quality input.

Data Architecture

So, finally, we come on to Data Architecture. Data Architecture is where it all gets a little real, both metaphorically and physically.

Data Architecture is the way in which data flows through an organisation, what is plumbed from what to where. It covers the structure of the data (the data model), the structure of databases, the way in which they are all linked together, how the information in data stores gets there in the first place, and how it gets from the data stores to end consumers.

If we are looking at enterprise data architecture as a discipline (and we should) this includes both the design of data architecture (the plumbing) and also the work to create and maintain the models, policies, rules, and standards – in fact anything that tries to get the data to the right place at the right time.

Data Architecture (the plumbing) is the landscape within which all the other disciplines operate. It is the means of implementation of the data strategy, and the way in which we serve our data dish to our customer. In our analogy it is the restaurant layout and kitchen size, the number of hobs on the oven and the number of shelves in the fridge. It is the number of tables and their layout, the table and tablecloth, the knives and forks and the plate.

Putting it all together?

It should be clear at this point that the various disciplines must work together for the betterment of the whole. Not only that, but because the whole is more than the sum of the parts, organisations that avoid investment in one are losing the combined upside.

For example, the practice of Data Governance creates a Data Strategy which will be delivered through Data Architecture. Trying to design a Data Architecture without a Data Strategy is trying to cook food to an unspecified order. What you end up with may be edible, but is unlikely to meet the customer requirements without a lot of luck.

The job of Data Governance, apart from the creation of the data strategy, is largely to design and monitor the practice of Data Management, and put in place a framework so that deviations are picked up on a timely basis. If the practice of Data Management is not doing its job, then it is the job of Data Governance to ensure it does.

Data Architecture must be business-orientated and business-aware. To do otherwise risks wasting money. Data Governance provides that link via the data strategy.

If the business wants near real time data, then this will have implications on the data architecture. If the business wants a place where they can query fifty years of claim history (underwriting, for example), then such a place needs to exist.

There is also a feedback loop. Like any landscape, the data architecture constrains the way in which those that use it can operate, but the difference here is that the landscape can be changed. If the day to day practice of data management identifies problems in the nature of the data deliverable this can result in changes to the data landscape being made for the better.

If the kitchen is too far from the tables the food will be cold on delivery. However this can be changed – admittedly not without some building work and re-plumbing, but it can be done.

Summary

The most important take-away point from this chapter is that there is a strong relationship between all data disciplines. All act together to ensure that the job is done correctly and that the business decision-makers get the information they need. Equally, each discipline has a different role:

- Data Architecture (the plumbing) is the landscape within which data operates and exists. Data Architecture (the discipline) designs and controls that landscape.
- Data Governance acts at a high level to keep control and make sure everything is done correctly.
- Data Management is the day to day operations.
- Data Quality is the aim.
- Data Strategy is how we get there.

I think the restaurant analogy used above helps promote understanding here. "Data" is an ambiguous and much-misused term. Substitution of food as the deliverable for the enterprise allows for a clear distinction to be made between the deliverable and the mechanisms – and governance – used to deliver it.

I would hope that it also shows how vital each data discipline is to ensure that the data deliverable is of good quality.

Chapter 4: Data Architecture (The Plumbing)

> *"An information ecosystem is a system with different components, each serving a community directly while working in concert with other components to provide a cohesive, balanced information environment."*
>
> Corporate Information Factory, W.H. Inmon et al, Wiley and Sons, 2001

Introduction

So, having had a brief overview, lets start to delve into the detail. The previous chapter outlined that:

■ Data Architecture (the plumbing) is the way in which information flows around the organisation. What is plumbed from where to where.

■ Data Architecture (the discipline) is the effort to control it – the design, the models, policies, rules, standards, etc. Anything that designs the pipework and tries to get the contents (the data) to the right place at the right time.

■ The Data Architect being the person who does one to try and control the other.

In this chapter I'll cover the plumbing and the concept of the information factory and information flow in more detail, and also translate that into the information needs of the organisation. I will cover "What is data?" "Why does it have to flow?" "Why can't we have one system that has everything in it?" "Who uses data, and why?"

What was brilliant about Inmon's concept of the information factory quoted at the start of this chapter is that it is so *right*. If we consider a factory for physical products, we instantly have a mental image of a production line, where raw materials are introduced at one end and finished product loaded into delivery vehicles at the other. The various parts of the factory are connected by conveyor belts, and something different occurs to the product at every stage, from component manufacture to finishing.

And so it is with data. Information flows through an organisation from the initial contact of a customer to a contact centre or branch through applications and data warehouses to end user reports, board reports and potentially a regulator. Key to data architecture is the understanding of this flow, understanding its component parts, and understanding how they interact.

Before "Information Technology" existed, data flow existed. 100 years ago orders were received from customers in paper format. These orders were received and copied, one copy being sent to the warehouse for picking (or the factory floor for manufacture), another copy went to finance. When the goods were dispatched, the dispatch note was matched to the invoice and the customer was invoiced.

In a very real way, *information flow* has not changed for hundreds of years, Information Technology has made it quick and easier, but the basics are still there.

Over time information systems were linked together, and data architecture was born. The order system linked to the factory, and the accounting system linked to the bank. Further evolution linked all the systems, and then built reporting systems on top. The Internet made everything faster and more complicated. Customers could enter orders digitally, which were automatically fulfilled and the only time a human came into the line would be at packing and dispatch.

An organisation is an information factory. It is complex and interconnected. If we ignore that complexity and refuse to understand its components we will never solve any data problem.

However, you could argue - and argue correctly - that data systems and organisations have moved on since Inmon wrote his book. So why is the concept of information flow still relevant now? The reason is the nature of information systems. Data systems have specialisms. To continue the factory analogy, some parts of information systems are good at processing raw materials, some are good at putting the finishing touches and making it look pretty. Rarely, if ever, are different components good at the same job.

Why Do We Need A Factory?

As this is an introductory chapter aiming to establish concepts, a key question to cover is why data flows in the first place. If information didn't need to flow then the need for the discipline of data architecture would be much reduced. But data needs to move from one place to another. Why?

Here we have to introduce some data fundamentals. I will go into more detail later in the book and explain the concepts and building blocks. At this high level, however, I will cover:

- Types of Data
- Types of Users
- Types of Architectural Construct

Types of Data

In most organisations there are four types of data:

- Customer Data
- Product Data
- Transaction Data
- Reference Data

I will cover each in turn.

Data on Customers

This itself is sub-divided into a number of different types. It is important for the Data Architect to know and be able to recognise different types of customer data, as the way the different types are treated, both in practice and especially in law, varies wildly, and for good reason.

- Some data will be an identifier which may or may not be unique, and may be changeable. For example, customer name.
- Some data will be inherent to the individual and unique and unchangeable, like biometric data (fingerprints and similar).
- Some data will be inherent to the individual and shared with others (hair colour).

- Some will relate to the individuals preferences. For example - consents and political views.
- Other information can cover location - address for example, or even current geographical position.
- Still other information covers relationships with others, and information on career - education, current employment, salary.

Depending on the products delivered by the organisation any or all of this information may be relevant and its all linked to a customer.

Data on customers may also be categorised a number of other ways.
- The concept of "Personally identifiable information" (PII Data) is important as it is referred to in law. Several regulations cover specifically this kind of data. A name is PII, a hair colour is not.
- "Sensitive" data is as described - data that would or could cause embarrassment or repercussions if lost or exposed. Health data is typically classed as "sensitive", however in some jurisdictions "political views" may also be considered sensitive.

Data on Products

Data that describes the products that the organisation sells or produces. This information typically doesn't change rapidly, simply because product change often involves a process that will include competitor and market analysis. Many levels of the organisation may be involved and there is often a signoff required from senior management. The organisation needs to ensure that the product is right for the organisation - in terms of its ability to deliver - and also right for the market in which it is being launched. As such it could be considered semi-static data.

Examples of this kind of data could be:
- Information on individual products in a warehouse. This could include a description, bar code/serial/product number. It could also include more detailed product information such as exact measurements or even a blueprint on how to construct it. It could also include price.
- It could be a prospectus of university courses. this could include the details of each course and who is teaching it. It could include the duration, subjects covered and qualifications obtained as a result of successful completion.

- Details of a mortgage. This could include rate, but also criteria, acceptable loan-to-value ratios, the amount of funding available for the overall mortgage pot, and duration of the offer.

This kind of data will vary according to the industry. In industries where the product is a commodity it may be common across organisations, but this is generally not the case, and product data is individual to the organisation.

Data on Transactions

Transaction data is a historical record, generally made at the time of the action itself, of an agreement made between two parties to buy or sell or otherwise interact.

Details of transactional data could include:
- withdrawals from a bank branch
- invoices relating to purchases
- contact centre records of conversations
- payments in a supermarket
- withdrawals from pharmaceutical stores in a hospital
- dispenses in an optical practice
- share trading sales and purchases
- ......and many others.

In short, a transaction is a historical record of something that has occurred. Typically transaction information is at a very granular level, containing detailed information on what happened at what time, and with what value.

There is a much higher volume of transaction data than other types of data. Whilst customers may number in the thousands, and products in the hundreds, transaction data, even in a relatively small organisation, can number in the tens or hundreds of thousands. In large organisations with many small transactions it can easily number in the billions.

For the Data Architect, the solution for transaction data may be very different from the relatively small scale data in other areas. Different types of database may have to be used where scalability is a prime concern.

Reference Data

Lastly, we cover reference data. Reference data is typically almost static, and is generally data that you would want to manage centrally. Examples may include:

- country codes
- country names and static data such as the currency applicable to a country, its area, or population
- organisational hierarchy
- industry data
- standard conversation tables
- human resources data such as who reports to what department

In short, reference data is characterised by being applicable across the organisation, and used by everyone. It also often refers to types of data that are external to the organisation and not under its control.

Typically this kind of data is used in - for example - drop down lists for customers to choose which country in which they are based. Having a central reference data set to which all drop-down lists refer, means that in the rare event of a change, one modification to the mater table in the reference data repository will change all drop-down lists across the organisation. This is far less risky than changes having to be made manually across hundreds of systems.

In the same way, standard conversions are better input once into a reference data set and used across an organisation than hard coded into every application as someone, somewhere, will make a mistake.

Types of Users

Next I will discuss the typical users of data. If we consider that the mission of a data architect is to ensure that the right data gets to the right people so they can make the right decisions, then who are these people? Ultimately these are the people that will be the consumers of data architecture.

Typically users divide into those that need detailed information at the most granular level, and those that typically use aggregated data. Another way of thinking about it is broad data sets - where users need all the data for one very specific area, or narrow, where users need a small subset of data for all the areas.

In reality, despite the broad brush categories I have used below, there are many types of users. This is becoming more the case as data use cases diverge and become increasingly specialised in today's data-driven organisations.

Operational Users

Operational users have the need for fast access to granular customer, product and transaction data. Operational users are the face of the organisation, and directly interact with customers and often suppliers. They need to know exactly which transaction the customer is querying – and to be able to view the details. They need to be able to see which invoice, and every detail of that invoice.

Generally, operational users have the most power over the data. They have the ability to directly change it, and are often the only ones who have that power. The operational users are also about the only users within the organisation who need actual up-to-the-second real time information.

Fraud

Despite the above, there is one other type of user who needs to see real time information, and that is the part of the organisation that is dealing with fraud and financial crime. The reason is fraudulent transactions need to be identified as soon as possible so that – hopefully - they can be stopped, hence limiting loss to both customers and the organisation.

IT Power Users and Auditors

About the only people who can see more data than operational users are the IT system administrators and the auditors. They need to see data such as "which operational user modified this record, and when" or "when was this query submitted and how long did it take to run."

It should be noted that there is a difference between being able to see data and modify it. Operational users can modify data. High level sysadmins generally should not be able to as part of their normal role.

It is also worth mentioning that privileged access accounts are normally tightly controlled. Most organisations strictly limit the number of accounts that have the high-level permissions to make changes to data, or see all the data in an organisation (for example, database administrators). These accounts are carefully monitored, and only given to those whose experience and ability mitigates the risk that having such power brings.

Management

The next stage up in terms of granularity is management. Management almost never need to see the individual records, but do need to see aggregated information. How many calls per day? How many products sold? Turnover per day? The actual level of aggregation required will be dependent on the level of management – a team leader will see day to day and month to month for their local team. The CEO will probably not look closer than week to week but will see the whole company. Here we again revisit the concept of "broad vs deep."

Analytics

Analytics users are the power users of data in the organisation. They will bring together every element of data – no matter how small – to look for patterns, to analyse and to guide the organisation. However, analytics users don't generally need to see data rapidly. Whilst many business users ask for real-time analytics, analytics is not, generally, time-critical. Analytics users sift and combine data sets – they are not generally expected to do this within a microsecond of the data becoming available.

Regulator

The requirements of the regulator vary widely depending on the industry. Although on a day to day basis, a regulator may only require aggregated reports – much in the manner of management – there is an increasing trend for regulators to require extremely granular transaction information so they can make their own mind up regarding the performance of the organisation. I have seen requirements for a report of every transaction per day to be sent to a regulator, and this is becoming more common.

In addition, if there is any kind of regulatory investigation, the regulator may well request system or audit logs, so in reality a regular may access any information in any organisation.

Customers

Finally, of course, there are customers. Customers want to see granular data, but generally only in a very narrow field – the data about themselves (customer profile) and their transactions (both historical and in-flight). They don't need – and should not have access to – aggregated data. They also – together with operational users – have the highest time-criticality. If they place an order they expect to be able to view that order immediately.

Architectural Building Blocks

Moving on from types of data and types of users, we move on to the architectural building blocks. The machinery and the conveyor belts within the factory. As mentioned earlier, there is an entire section of the book that covers this in detail, however a little explanation is necessary so that I can move on to explain the way that data flows, and, importantly, *why* it has to flow.

The main building blocks in our information factory are:

- Operational systems - the core systems that are at the heart of any organisation. They ingest raw information from customer interactions, and use this information to process and store transactions. Without these systems the organization cannot function, cannot make money, cannot service customers. They must not break down.

- Data movement systems. These are the conveyors moving information from one place to another. They may move information in the manner of a conveyor belt – continuously moving a small bit at a time – or in the manner of a hopper or lorry delivery – large amounts at intervals.

- Data storage systems: These come in different kinds:
  - Back end databases store data for operational systems. Generally these are short term but high detail.
  - Operational Data Stores are short term analytics and reporting data stores.
  - Data Warehouses are data stores that are designed to hold large amounts of data at both high detail, and long term.
  - Data Marts are specialized data stores that present data for one area of the organization.

- ■ Reporting and Analytics systems. These systems do not directly serve customers but will perform large-scale analytics to identify insights to improve the business, create reports to management, or the regulator. They may provide "canned reports" – pre-programmed to give the same output each time – or may undertake one-off deep analysis of the data. They may also act to present data in a way that is user-friendly (for example systems that specialise in visualisation of data sets).

All are essential, but equally, all are different parts of the factory.

Fundamentals of Data Flow

So, we have briefly covered the data, the users, and basic architecture building blocks. This allows us enough background to cover the next concept, which is key to the whole of the data architecture discipline. Why does data need to flow? Why do we have a factory? Why can't we just have a large system that does everything. Surely it would be easier, cheaper and a lot less complicated?

The reason comes down to fundamentals of data and systems.

Some things just have to be separated, and many systems are designed for one purpose and not good at two different things. Let us use the example of wishing to build a car that will perform well in off-road rough terrain but can also achieve 250mph. With current technology it just doesn't exist. The reason is because the requirements of one (for example high ground clearance) naturally exclude the solution for the other (a ground-hugging form with its requirements based from aerodynamics).

Technology is specialised in different ways and the requirements of one exclude the solution for the other. However both requirements are needed, so two systems are needed, each one specialised for a different requirement. These systems have to interact, so we have to transport data between them. Data has to flow, and we suddenly have the concept of data architecture.

Of course, if this was the only constraint, we'd have two systems, and that would be it. But even in the best designed organisations there are often many more than that. Why is this the case? Well, this is because of some more fundamentals.

- The first is that you should *not* perform reporting and analytics from operational product fulfillment systems. The operational product fulfillment systems are systems directly serving customers, processing orders and transactions. Reporting and analytics are demanding workloads, and the last thing anyone wants is customers to be not able to buy anything because someone in marketing has run a report and swiped all the processing power available. So separation of operational fulfillment systems and reporting/analytics is a necessity.

- The second fundamental is the differing nature of operational and reporting systems. Operational systems receive data from a user interface (web, mobile, branch, etc) and write this to a back end database. Reporting systems take data from a database, manipulate it and export it to a user interface. So operational systems generally *write* data, reporting systems generally *read* data. Here we have the problem mentioned above. Writing data and reading data are different specialisms, requiring different data structures. Operational systems structure the data for optimal performance for write. Reporting systems optimise the structures for read.

- The third fundamental issue is history. Most operational systems don't keep years of data history. They keep the minimum set relevant to the product lifecycle, and offload when it is no longer current work in progress. The reason is again performance. If a customer cancels an order then the application doesn't want to look through 40 years of orders to find the right one to cancel. So there needs to be a place to offload historical data that isn't in operational use anymore.

- The fourth fundamental is selection of necessary data. When it comes to reporting and analytics then you want to be working with the minimum data set that meets your requirements. If, for example, you are analysing trends for purchases, the location of the customer at the time of purchase may not be relevant. You don't want to have to manipulate unneeded data, as it will cause a performance hit. So your reporting systems need to have only the data that is relevant for you and your needs.

- The fifth fundamental is data "width." Operational data systems won't include all the data that may be useful for analytics. An ordering system for barbeques just needs to accept a customer order and process it. It doesn't need to know about the weather at the time of purchase. However analytics systems may absolutely want to know data about the weather.

- The sixth fundamental is the nature of whether systems need "true" or "certain" data. Many organisations use data that may or may not be true - for example a forecast of future sales, future weather or future stock prices. However to process an order a fulfilment system doesn't care what a customer may do in the future – it just needs to know what the customer wants now. Speculation forms no part of its makeup. However, to continue the above analogy, the future weather prediction for next summer is absolutely required information for the BBQ maker predicting demand, but that data may – or may not – be very accurate. So we need to separate data that is true from data that "may" be true.

- The seventh fundamental is system constraint. Whether systems need to be open and flexible, or whether they are tightly defined. Analytics systems draw data from many systems. This data may be different formats and types. Analytics users manipulate this data, match it, and work with it. This is computationally expensive, and requires flexibility in the ability to store and manipulate data. However operational systems just need to store the data they work with, and do this quickly to keep up with customer needs and the needs of the organisation. The tighter defined and constrained the system is, the lower the risk, and (generally) the faster the performance.

- The eight fundamental is certainty of use. Operational systems know what they are using the data for. Analytics systems generally don't. They know data ingested might be useful, on the other hand it may not. Operational systems are not designed to deal with unknowns. They are designed to do one job, and do it well.

- The ninth fundamental is accuracy. Operational systems need to know their data is accurate. Analytics data may, or may not be, accurate. A customer order must be held in systems as fact. However an analytics system may have interpretative data - one customer *may* be related to another customer, or *may* be wishing to buy a certain product based on their purchases of other products. Operational systems neither have the interest or the capacity to run these analytics workloads.

■ The tenth fundamental is Access. Analytics systems need human access, operational systems need as little access as possible. Ideally almost no-one has direct access to operational systems. The risk is too high. All interaction is performed by system to system interactions which are very carefully controlled. Human beings make errors, and most businesses cannot allow their operational systems to be brought down by a mis-typed command.

Summary

A typical organisation therefore has many areas of data need.

■ Operational systems, tightly controlled, insulated from the rest of the organisation, outward facing, focused on serving customers.
■ Reporting systems, more open access, will combine many data sets.
■ An archive that holds all of the operational data for ever – or as long as is necessary.

Data needs to flow between such systems. No one system can meet all requirements. So data architecture needs to exist.

Chapter 5: Types of Data Architect

Introduction

If the understanding of information flow is critical for the organisation, it follows that so is the discipline and role that controls and curates it. As I said in the introduction:

■ Data Architecture (the plumbing) is the way in which information flows around the organisation. What is plumbed from where to where.

■ Data Architecture (the discipline) is the effort to control it – the design, the models, policies, rules, standards, etc. Anything that designs pipework and tries to get its contents (the data) to the right place at the right time.

■ The Data Architect being the person who does one to try and control the other.

Having covered - at a high level - the information flow, I will now move on to the discipline and roles.

This chapter will start by covering the different types of data architect. Architects at more senior levels are very much concerned with strategy and governance, whereas architects assigned to individual projects will concentrate on a much smaller scope, and a much shorter timescale.

The two subsequent chapters will cover two specific disciplines and roles. That of Enterprise Data Architecture, the more senior and least detailed of the disciplines, but with the widest scope, and that of Project Data Architecture, the (generally) less senior, but more detailed. I will not cover the other data architecture roles as they are variations on a theme, with the domain data architect sitting roughly between the two, with some of the responsibilities of both.

Types of Data Architect

Chief Data Architect

The Chief Data Architect would typically lead data architecture for an entire organisation. Their role is to define the design of data flow across the organisation. They are typically much less technical than other data architects, and may well be concerned more with data strategy, integration of data architecture with other data functions such as the Chief Data Office or data management, and managing the data architecture team.

The "Chief Data Architect" is essentially the most senior of the enterprise data architects, and leads that team. Hence a part of the role is concerned with general (non-data) management responsibilities such as HR, budgets, and similar.

The Chief Data Architect will also have other control responsibilities. In many organisations a key role is controlling the data flow, and part of controlling that data flow is to design controls and exercise control over how that data flow is built. It is this latter role that is different for the Chief Data Architect than other, non-enterprise architects.

Architecture controls can take many forms. That is a discussion for a later chapter.

Lastly, the Chief Data Architect has the final word on data designs. They are the "court of appeal" and will be the final arbiter where there is disagreement on data design.

Enterprise Data Architect

The Enterprise Data Architect is concerned about data flow throughout the organisation. There is no part of the organisation that is outside their remit. Their role is to consider the organisation as a unit.

The difference between the Enterprise Data Architect and the Chief Data Architect is they don't (generally) have management responsibilities - they are not responsible for the data architecture team. They can therefore dedicate their time to data architecture, rather than the management responsibilities.

If the Chief Data Architect's role is to approve, the Enterprise Data Architect's role is to create. An Enterprise Data Architect will cover:

- Writing standards for data, data modelling, data controls, data tooling.
- Setting strategy for architecture, and designing - at a macro level - that architecture.
- Liaising with external third parties, understanding new developments in the market, what is new and how it can help the organisation.
- Working with other parts of the organisation to develop and agree data architecture.
- Dealing with problems that are escalated from lower levels of architecture.

Domain Data Architect

The Domain Data Architect sits between the Enterprise Data Architect and the Project Architect. As a result it is no surprise that their role is a little bit of both.

Their role is to curate the data flow within a defined area of the organisation. This may be a division, or a country, or a product - whatever is appropriate to the company organisation. The domain data architect will have responsibility for a number of projects, and will support the project architects in their work.

They take the standards created by Enterprise Architects and help to implement them.

Project Data Architect

The Project Data Architect is assigned to an individual project to cover the design of data and data structures within the individual project.

They would be expected to have knowledge of the wider organisation data architecture strategy and standards, so that they can align with the wider organisation in what is proposed for their project.

I will cover the role and responsibilities of the project data architect in a later chapter.

Why do we need Data Architects?

An important question to answer is why should we have a data architect in the first place? Why have a specialist to cover this particular role to design and curate the flow within the information factory?

We need a specialist because information factories are complex. Data flows in even relatively small organisations are extremely complex and the design, governance and management of it absolutely deserves the attention of a specialist.

In addition the specialist needs to know about not only the nuts and bolts of the machines in the factory, but also the reason why the product is being built. To continue the analogy, a smear of oil may be perfectly acceptable for a machine part, and unacceptable for food. So they need to know a bit about nuts and bolts, a bit about requirements, a lot about the transformation of the material as it moves through the factory and a clear understanding of how the various conveyor belts interconnect.

Once we have accepted that there is someone - not fully business and not fully IT - who needs to worry about data flow, then we need to consider how hard a job it will be. In reality, the complexity is huge.

A typical organisation may have hundreds of data sources. These will populate data aggregation warehouses via thousands of feeds, and then secondary functions such as risk, finance, analytics, MI and so on will not only consume via many more hundreds of feeds, but will also create their own data. In large organisations there may be hundreds of thousands of applications and millions of data movements, each of which may consist of hundreds or thousands of data items. This is a level of complexity higher than most other professionals need to understand.

Examples of data, where it comes from and where it goes, may include:

- Website – applications and orders input, and analytics of visits
- Website back end databases – applications and order storage
- Contact centre – customer interaction data including voice recordings, and applications and orders
- Mobile app – applications, orders and customer interaction

- Core systems – transactions
- Payments systems – payments (in and out)
- Physical warehouse and product systems – orders fulfilled, products in/ out, stock
- Finance systems – accounts, profitability
- Risk systems – risk appetite
- Analytics and MI systems – product performance, personnel performance, insights and reports

The data that enters the organisation though the customer touchpoint is exactly the same underlying data that underpins the annual accounts and decisions on dividends to shareholders.

That understanding of flow is what is critical to organisational data success, and it is the key skill that data architects bring to the table. There is generally, no-one else – apart from the Data Architect – who thinks of the flow of data through the organisation.

The IT/Business Problem

Unfortunately, there are a lot of misconceptions and sometimes the data professional will be challenged with the view, from either IT or the business, that a data architect is not needed. As a result I will expand on the earlier short explanation as to why this view exists, mostly so the data architect can understand and counter the arguments. A sales role is often part of the data architect's day job.

The misconceptions around data architecture exist on both the business and IT side of many organisations.

The IT perspective

From an IT perspective, it is the business that provide and own the data - after all it is the business that are interacting with the customer and the customer provides the data. All IT do is move it around.

A common presumption is that functionality is more important than data. Developers write code, and this code supports applications or user interfaces that are presented to the customer, or have capabilities that perform functions.

It is often forgotten that critical to all functions is the data that supports it – data that the applications, the user interfaces and the code move around. Moreover, most IT projects deal with a single function. It has data inputs and data outputs, but that's about as far as is considered – the project functions in a silo.

Data is, at best, something that is used to test the application is working as intended. The data itself - how it flows - is not a consideration. Many applications have negative impacts on the data as a result.

The business perspective

From the business side the common perception is that the data is a technology construct. IT owns the data and "provides" it to the rest of the organisation. The concept of data flow doesn't really exist. An assumption exists from business users that the data is held in the front end systems, because that's what they see. That the front end connects to a far-off database via multiple linkages isn't really thinking that occurs.

To illustrate, its a bit like saying "the water is in the tap" - no, actually, the tap is where you access the water, but actually the water you use is a continuously moving pipeline.

You can see by the tap analogy how easy it is to fall into this kind of thinking - how many people, when they turn on a tap, think of the far-off reservoir that is getting lower by fractions of a millimetre? But this concept of flow is integral to the role of a data architect.

Therefore from the business side data is often seen as an "IT thing" that is "technical" and therefore outside their control and interest. They think about customer, and profit, and costs, and data doesn't relate to any of these. Of course, in reality, data underpins it all, but that's not how people think.

In the series "Hitchhikers Guide to the Galaxy" Douglas Adams coined the idea of making something invisible with a "Somebody Else's Problem" field. This is where data sits in many organisations. IT think its a business problem, The business think it is an IT problem.

Sadly it is very easy for both sides to come to the conclusion that the "other side" owns the data and for the data to fall down a black hole. This is the reason for the rise in the role of "Chief Data Officer." If you look at the words themselves then "Chief Information Officer" means more or less exactly the same thing, but in reality many CIOs confine themselves to thinking primarily about technology, not information.

In order to fill a gap, the concept of a data specialist has arisen. This specialist is concerned with data flow. This specialist is the Data Architect.

What Benefit Does Data Architecture bring?

So what value does the Data Architect bring?

- The Data Architect often acts as a "translator" between business and IT. A Data Architect naturally has abilities in both areas.
- Projects are implemented more quickly, with less frustration, less blind alleys, and less trail and error.
- Productivity of both a project team, and, at the enterprise level, the organisation, is increased.
- The product is better. It better meets requirements, but not just that, its quality is better. This applies whether the product is a report or the information flow through the organisation as a whole.
- Costs are significantly reduced. This is not just "costs to create" but also "costs to run."
- Understanding is increased. Understanding of the challenge of data, and understanding of how to get it right.
- Future projects are likely to run more effectively, and a positive feed-back loop is created, where understand and learning achieved by project members is used again and again.

All of this might appear a little too positive, but it is all effects of a design specialist being involved in a change scenario. We wouldn't build a bridge without a structural engineer, we would assume that the bridge would fall down. So why do organisations try and build data constructs without a data specialist?

Up front design in complex system is essential. The Data Architect is the designer of information systems, who will not only design, but will shepherd change from start to completion.

Summary

In this chapter I have covered the various types of Data Architect, and explained how roles differ. I have explained why we need Data Architects, and why they are needed in an organisation.

In reality, Data Architects are essential members of both a project team and of the organisation as a whole.

Next I will delve into the role of Enterprise and Project Data Architects, explain the disciplines and what they would be doing on a day to day basis.

Chapter 6: Enterprise Data Architecture

Introduction

I stated in the earlier chapter that Data Architecture disciplines and roles operate at many different levels in any organisation.

Enterprise Data Architecture happens at the macro level, at the top of the organisation. It is concerned with longer term, it is less technical. It typically requires a lot of interaction with Executives, as well as other key stakeholders like the Chief Data Officer, the Chief Technical Officer and the Chief Operating Officer. It may be aligned with technology, or it may sit across technology and business.

Position and Reporting Lines

The Enterprise Data Architect is generally a senior position. There are three main patterns.

- Reporting to the Chief Architect, alongside other Enterprise Architects. The Chief Architect reports to the Chief Information Officer (CIO).
- Reporting to the Chief Enterprise Architect, or, for Enterprise Data Architects, the Chief Data Architect.
- Reporting to the Chief Data Officer (CDO)

Exactly which will depend on the responsibilities and roles at the top of the organisation, and there are many more variants than the above. These are just the most common. I have seen Data Architects reporting to business leaders, Chief Control Officers, Chief Operational Officers, Chief Risk Officers, and many other options. It is worth noting that - of course - the reporting line of the Data Architect - or the CDO for that matter - can say a lot about the approach to data in an organisation, and how seriously it is taken. If the reporting line is far from the organisation's centre of control then it is likely that any data initiatives will feel a little uphill.

What does the Discipline and Role involve?

Although the two disciplines of Project and Enterprise Data Architecture interact there is much difference between them. Its a bit like the difference between driving a bicycle and driving a truck. Whilst both technically involve roads, and there is some crossover, there's much unique to each endeavour.

In this chapter and the next I will give an overview of the two disciplines. I will start with Enterprise Data Architecture.

I used the analogy about riding a bicycle and driving a truck. Enterprise Data Architecture is definitely the truck. It's difficult to steer, doesn't accelerate or stop quickly, and can have disastrous consequences for the organisation if it goes wrong.

There are two main focus areas:

- There is the "future focus" where Enterprise Data Architecture will describe the future state of data flow in the organisation and guide the organisation on how to get there.
- There is the "current focus" where Enterprise Data Architecture will create standards to ensure consistency of approach across the organisation and help govern the change happening now.

Future and Outward Focus

The Data Architecture Strategy

The first task for Enterprise Data Architecture is setting long term Data Architecture strategy. This involves taking a wide understanding of the existing estate, and knowledge of the business pain points, the legal and regulatory timeline and the knowledge of industry standards, competitor activity and offerings by external vendors and designing a future state data architecture for the organisation that is implementable, practical, affordable and effective.

It is clear that all of the above require a deep level knowledge of the organisation, the data flows through it and a clear understanding of where the business needs to be in the future. It is for this reason Enterprise Data Architecture is not a technology-only discipline, but needs to understand business as well.

- For example, if the business strategy is to divest a division, or stop making a certain product, then the architect needs to design systems that allow a modular disconnect of that division.

- The architect needs to consider what will information flow look like in 5 years time? In 10 years time? Is the current state of information flow constraining the organisation, and will the organisation need to change its information flow from current state?

- If there is change required, what is the target state, and why? How is the organisation going to achieve that target state. If it is not "big bang" (change everything all at once) then what will be the transition states, and what will they involve? If we are to have transition states, what are the dependencies between the various transition states? What needs to happen first, and why?

- The Enterprise Data Architect also requires a deep knowledge of the existing information pain points. Where are problems now? What ways can they be solved?

In short, the Enterprise Data Architect needs to bring a holistic view of the present and the future together, to create a strategy for the organisation to work to.

I will now set out the key considerations of the strategy. What are we trying to achieve with the strategy? How does this link in with Data Architecture?

Improving Change Efficiency and Agility

A key component of the strategy is improving change efficiency and agility.

A significant upside to an organisation having a good data architecture is agility. This means being able to change quickly in response to a changing market, changing circumstances, or because of disruptive effects of competitors. Ability to change is a key strategic need that most executives will easily recognise. In many markets – especially fast moving ones or those based on technology – inability to change is an existential threat to the organisation.

Poor data architecture makes it incredibly difficult for the business to change in response to its market.

If you can imagine an organisation where data flows are a web of unknown complexity, managing change is difficult. How do you remove a division when its data is used by every other division? How to you add a product when you have to create new customer data because you cannot rely on what you already have? Modular parts facilitate change. Linking everything together so you cannot change one part without changing a dozen others impairs it.

When justifying a data architecture capability this is relatively easy to explain and most executives will "get it." Complexity breeds fragility.

Minimising Legal and Regulatory Risk

Another component of the strategy is managing legal and regulatory risk. Poor data architecture brings with it legal and regulatory risk. This is a subject very close to the hearts of business executives – no-one wants a large regulatory fine on their watch. By why is poor data architecture such an issue?

I shall give an example. If data is spread all over the organisation and no-one know where to find it, then the organisation is unable to govern it. So if a regulation arises covering data privacy for personal data – GDPR, for example – than the organisation cannot comply without first undertaking a huge exercise to find out where personal data is stored.

A second example might be a regulatory question around protecting customer data. Or a regulator might ask the organisation to prove that the figures in their annual report are from a "trusted source" and to demonstrate data lineage.

An organisation with good data architecture will be able to rapidly answer regulatory enquiries, and provide figures that inspire confidence. If the regulator asks for a report and the answer is "we will have to go and find out where all the data is, please come back in six months" - it is not a good look.

Its been said before that an organisation that cannot govern its data architecture will never know where its data is, or whether it is correct. An organisation that does not know where its data is, or whether it is correct, is not in control.

Understanding and Controlling IT and Business Costs

Another consideration of the strategy is controlling and minimising the cost of both business and IT. This is because poor, complex architecture will cost more to maintain than a more streamlined one. From an IT perspective, duplication of data stores will duplicate the costs to maintain them. Duplication of data movements results in more to go wrong, and a greater chance of failure, as well as higher loads on source systems and greater costs to support the complexity.

However, it is not just IT affected. A typical problem caused by poor data architecture is business end users spend as much time working out whether the data they are using is right as actually doing their work. It is common for business users to perform "pre-work" cleaning, matching and preparing data, and this effort can be a substantial part of their time.

The reason? Complex data architecture, where data is being pulled from different places or at different times.

This is one of the most frustrating causes of high operational business cost, because it is so preventable. However if professional staff do not trust data they use to make decisions then they will take steps to determine the quality of data, work out data lineage and establish that trust themselves.

This lack of trust may stem from different definitions used in different departments, or, often multiple databases with different information – no "single version of the truth." In fact, lack of trust may cause a problem even when there is little wrong with the data. Relatively minor data quality issues may still cause staff to expend considerable effort to corroborate the system-produced data.

On the other hand a well-architected organisation has a clear, clean source of data which everyone can use.

Anecdote

The financial controller of a large organisation once stated to me that his staff were spending 80% of their time cleansing data and 20% of their time using it.

Ensuring Data Quality

One of the key effects of poor data architecture is poor data quality. So a consideration in the strategy is making sure data is right.

Poor data quality causes many significant business issues. These can include:

- Cost of poor decisions
- Issues with risk and capital management
- Poor relations between IT and the Business
- Mis-targeted marketing
- Reputational impacts
- Poor customer relations and customer retention
- Issues fighting crime and terrorism
- Transactional failures
- IT project failures
- Lower profitability
- Unable to identify regulatory breaches

In short, poor data quality can cost an organisation a very large amount of money.

The quality of the data is often seen as outside their role by many data architects, especially those that are more technically focused. There can be a perception that the job of a data architect is to move the data around, not to care about its quality.

However I feel this is an incorrect view. If the job of the data architect is to get "the right data to the right place at the right time" then quality is an integral part of the role. Equally, the quality of the data is significantly dependent on the quality of the data architecture. The strategy needs to consider this.

- Example 1: If poor architecture means that data is held in two places, then a change may only be applied to one of them. The data is then out of sync, and in future knowing which of two values for address is correct is extremely difficult.

- Example 2: If poor data design means that data movement technology drops or transforms data then the data received by the consumer may be incorrect, but the business may be unaware that data has changed from the original.

In short, the design of information flow needs to care about quality in the same way that design of water flow needs to ensure that it is not polluted - or lost - on its journey.

Aligning with Industry Norms

Another important requirement of the strategy is to ensure alignment with industry norms and practices. This covers both new products, and best practice.

New products
Information technology is continuously evolving. Software providers create new products continually. Although many are evolutionary, some are revolutionary. The Enterprise Data Architect needs to keep an "ear to the ground" and understand which products are emerging in the marketplace, and equally, which products are being demised.

If, for example, a product currently in use by the organisation is going to be demised by the vendor and support is going to cease, the Enterprise Data Architect will need to plan an exit strategy.

Work in this area may include

- Meet with external vendors to understand their offerings, what they can bring to the organisation, and - importantly - how they intend to evolve in the future.

- Read trade press to keep abreast of any new techniques that are emerging in the industry that may help the organisation. Particularly relevant are the strategies and techniques used by start-ups and challengers, and how they differ from the organisation in question.

Best practice
The second area relevant to industry norms is best practice. This in itself covers a number of areas.

- Firstly, what are other organisations doing? Most organisations measure themselves against their peers - first quartile, second quartile, etc.

They may well differentiate this by market. "We need to be the best in this market, we are happy to simply match our peers in this market."

- Secondly, are there any industry standards, if so what are they, are they evolving, and how does the organisation measure up against them? Particularly in relation to data, common standards are:
    - DAMA (Data Management Association)
    - COBIT 9 (Information Systems and Governance Association)
    - DCAM (Data Management Council)

- Thirdly, what are the regulatory expectations? What are they now, which way are they heading? What are the interests of the regulator, and is there any information on what the regulator may require in terms of data in a year - or 5 years - time? Regulators will often have particular areas of interest, or be moving in a certain direction. Regulators may have positive or negative views on new technological developments. Knowing these helps the Enterprise Data Architect plan. Work here will involve meeting with representatives of regulatory, legal and compliance to understand changes to laws and regulations that may affect data.

- Fourthly, legal. Closely allied to regulatory, what laws are coming that will affect data? Legal changes are often known about years in advance so there is no excuse for the organisation to be caught on the hop. An example of laws that fundamentally affect data architecture are data residency laws. Many countries have passed laws that state that citizens data should not be hosted outside the country. If such a law is incoming, its possible that entire data structures will have to be lifted and shifted to a different country. If this is the case it needs to be planned well in advance, as such migrations are costly, difficult and complex. Doing them at the last minute vastly increases risk to the organisation. Again work here will involve meeting with representatives of regulatory, legal and compliance to understand what is coming.

Co-ordinating investment

Lastly within the strategy is co-ordination of investment. Many organisations will have many data projects in flight at the same time. Many of these may be trying to achieve the same goal.

The Enterprise Data Architect needs to understand the investment occurring across the organisation, and act to ensure that the same thing is not being built in multiple places, and that data is re-used as much as possible.

The same thing built in separate places is extremely common. In almost every organisation different divisions will build their own analytics data warehouse. This is wasteful in terms of resources, and significant savings can be made if the implementation is co-ordinated.

Such co-ordination is very hard to achieve. Most divisions wish to retain control of their own investment. Sharing of investment for the common good does not come easily. The data architecture function needs to be masters of persuasion and diplomacy.

The same applies to data sets. It is much easier for a project to build a single feed from a source system for their own personal consumption than share an existing one. However if every project does this then the result is many thousands of data feeds, and many will use the same data. So sharing really makes sense, and contrary to project expectations saves money, and speeds up delivery. Despite this, the challenge is often about political control and ownership. Again, diplomacy, persuasion and appealing to the common or greater good is a key skill of the Data Architect.

Current Focus

If the above is looking to the future of the organisation, I will now cover the capabilities of Enterprise Data Architecture that look to manage change that is occurring now.

Understanding the Organisation

The Enterprise Data Architect should be the subject matter expert on the data architecture in the organisation. This covers all areas - data flows, data stores, business data issues, and tooling. The Enterprise Data Architect needs to:

- Continuously work to understand the existing estate and how it works. This includes all data stores, the way in which data moves across the organisation, who uses data and its lineage. Essentially the Enterprise Data Architect should become the go-to person on data understanding.

- Understand business pain points. Meet with business users of data to find out what problems are and why. What things do they want to do with data but cannot? What are their pain points? This kind of meeting is critical for a number of reasons:
    - It informs strategy
    - It means the enterprise architect understands what is wrong with the organisation
    - It builds relationships with business
    - Business feel that their data issues are being taken seriously
    - Business may not try and solve the problem themselves with vast amount of end user computing that brings risk - and inaccuracy - to the organisation.

- Identify candidates within the estate for demise in order to simplify the estate and reduce overall run costs. Most organisations have many legacy applications that have few users but still cost money in terms of license fees and hardware support.

- Firedrills: Common and sometimes fun, sometimes not. The free dictionary describes firedrills as "an unexpected, hurried, chaotic task." It is usually an event where someone senior - or the regulator - needs information very fast and the Data Architect is drafted in because they know where the information is. An example may be "We've been asked to report on how many sources of customer data we have" or "how many systems do we have in the UK?" In short, its a drop-everything task with a ridiculous deadline. Depending on the organisation these can be rare or constant.

Risk and Controls

The next area the Enterprise Data Architect should understand is the control environment around data in the organisation. This will include the work to:

- Understand and assess data risk and data architecture risk. Understand how it can be identified and how it can be controlled. Propose methods of both measurement and control, and potentially execute on both.

- Understand data controls. Data controls will not necessarily be set by the data architect. However the data architect needs to understand data controls as they will massively overlap into the data architecture domain. Controlling data is a lot more difficult if the data architecture of the organisation is complex. Equally, controls won't work unless those responsible for setting controls understand the data architecture. Many controls are set assuming a data architecture that is much less complex than what exists in reality, and as a result controls fail to work effectively. The data architect can help at every level of data control. The data architect may in fact be the owner of some data controls, depending on how the organisation is structured.

- Develop new ways of governance. Governance, the need for it, and what it covers, is continuously changing. Regulators are becoming more interested in data, and laws are changing all the time, therefore governance is changing all the time. Governance has to be redesigned, and ideally the ever increasing need for governance should not create an ever increasing workload. Enterprise architects need to think about, and implement, smarter ways of dealing with the governance workload.

Creation of Standards

As mentioned in the previous chapter the Enterprise Data Architect needs to ensure that the organisation operates in a consistent manner, and a key part of that is defining standards that both meet the requirements for control and risk governance, but also can be applied consistently across the organisation by Project and Domain Data Architects.

The Enterprise Data Architect is limited in time, and in any organisation of any size, cannot sit with every project and explain requirements in detail. Whilst the Project Data Architects have the time, they need to be able to give consistent guidance, so each project in the organisation executes to the same standard.

So standards need to be defined both to ensure consistency and understanding. These will include:

- Architecture Patterns: A very effective way of governing architecture in an organisation is approved architecture patterns. Patterns are a library of pre-approved acceptable best practice architectures to be used within the organisation. The assumption is that project and domain architects will use patterns to inform their own designs, and follow them when possible. This then simplifies governance as designs following patterns would be essentially "pre-approved."

- Modelling Standards: Although a data architect is not a data modeller, Enterprise Data Architecture often becomes involved in setting modelling standards. If there is a Chief Data Modeller then this would of course be their role, but in most organisations modelling standards - which notation to use, what format, what level of granularity - are set by Enterprise Data Architecture.

- Data Model: Further to modelling standards, the creation of an enterprise data model often falls to Enterprise Data Architecture. It should be noted here that several organisations produce standard data models for many industries and these can be "bought-in." The model doesn't have to be created from scratch.

- Architecture Documentation Standards: How should architecture be documented? These standards cover which tooling is used, where documentation is held, what level of detail is required, and so on. Setting standards up front means you don't ask the same questions at every project meeting.

- Approval Guidelines: Defining levels of approval required for Project Data Architects. It is unlikely every data design needs to be approved by Enterprise Data Architecture, so there needs to be guidelines in place as to what needs to be approved, and by whom, and when, and what evidence is required for the approval submission. It also covers where the approval will be documented, what is a material change that would require an additional approval, where there are any time limits on approvals, and so on.

- Control standards: What controls are required for each project? The controls that are applicable for each project will often depend on the type of project. It is common, for example, for specific controls to be required if the solution passes data to a third party. With the prevalence of software-as-a-service and outsourcing of data functions, this is becoming more common. Control standards will typically cover:
  - Project Development
  - Data Integrity

- Data Privacy
- Data Security
- Data Architecture
- Data Management
- Data Sourcing
- Documentation of data dictionaries and data interfaces

- Evidence Standards: The evidence required to demonstrate that a project has followed appropriate process. This evidence allows a project to document that it has made the right decisions, and is often an essential compliance requirement for internal or external audit or a regulator. For example, has a project created a data flow diagram?

- Tooling Standards: Which tools are approved for use in the organisation? Data tooling governance is a key part of data architecture. Tooling governance ensures that license fees are kept under control, skills are transferable across the organisation, and the organisation doesn't end up using one proprietary format for reports in one division and a different format in another.

- Escalation Triggers: What are key triggers that will require escalation to Enterprise Data Architecture - or a senior architect? Common triggers may include the project design incorporating use of sensitive personal customer data (example - health records), or use of biometrics, or particular architectural solutions - which could be as specific as "use of a particular supplier." These escalation triggers are the red flags that a senior opinion is needed.

- Data Documentation Standards: Standards for documentation of the data itself. So, for example, if you are creating a data dictionary for an application, what information needs to be included, and to what detail?

- Data Requirements Standards: When a project architect defines data requirements it needs to be to a consistent standard across the organisation, and to a standard that makes it clear what is required, and hence a level that a design can be created to meet. The data requirements need to include information on what data is required, where it is required, and to what standard. They also need to cover the types of data, any special treatments required, and also expected transformations that may occur in the project. In short, everything "data" about the project needs to be specified before it is built. This applies whether the development is waterfall, agile or devops. All that changes is the timescale. Waterfall would cover design for the whole project. Agile for the next sprint.

Executing Governance and Giving Advice

Unfortunately, however many standards are written, or project patterns approved, there will always be exceptions which do not fit well. Here it is easier to meet with the business leaders and IT staff and discuss the problem and how it can be solved in a way that meets requirements but does not expose the organisation to risk. This work will include:

- Attending design authority meetings to review designs and offer the data perspective. This may well involve approving or stopping projects or deferring judgment until further investigation is completed, or approving with conditions.

- Design forums: An important role of the Enterprise Data Architect is the creation and running of design forums. These forums will typically consist of a number of senior subject matter experts who will review designs presented for approval. It is unlikely that every design will be presented, but only those which are exceptions to the established design patterns on the organization. The Enterprise Data Architect will need to:
  - Create terms of reference
  - Identify participants
  - Run and minute decisions made
  - Follow up

- Meeting with project architects and managers, understanding the project purpose and its business deliverables, and making a decision on whether the project meets enterprise standards across the board for:
  - Resilience
  - Strategic state
  - Non-functional requirements
  - Control adherence
  - Appropriate architecture
  - Peer review

- Engineering efficiency
- Meeting business benefit
- Governance - does the project need it?

- It should be noted that the above are often very challenging meetings. The Enterprise Data Architect needs to absorb a vast amount of information very quickly and make on-the-fly decisions.

- Act as a Subject Matter Expert for data design, advising solution architects and less experienced data architects in the design and delivery of data architectures for business solutions that balance flexibility and affordability but without compromising architectural integrity. This consultancy role is really important, and a key part of ensuring that problems are stopped from occurring. It is a lot easier to stop problems occurring in the first place than clean them up later. This also includes providing full data architecture life cycle guidance to business and IT teams to ensure quality technical deliverables.

- Support delivery teams in making the most of data technologies and helping them transition to strategic systems to optimise data related outcomes and roadmaps.

Building Community and Communication

Key to the success of data architecture is building community. A data architecture function cannot execute and realise its aims unless it integrates and links with the wider community of solution architects, project managers, business process owners, data governors and data stewards, and control and risk departments. In short, the enterprise data function needs to have high connectivity to the rest of the organisation. Examples of this may include:

- Solution Architects need to know what a good data architecture solution is, what good data patterns are, what is acceptable, what are trigger points.
- The Executive needs to understand and support data architecture.
- CDOs need to know the good work that enterprise data architecture is doing.
- CCOs need to understand the controls that data architecture supports.

- Business Analysts needs to understand what good data requirements look like.
- Control Owners need to understand how data architecture will affect the risk to the organisation.
- Data Governors need to understand how data architecture will facilitate their own role.
- Business Process Owners need to understand the data architecture that underpins their processes, what constraints and opportunities the data architecture gives them, and what are their architectural risk points.

It is the nature of data architecture that many more people are doing data architecture than there are data architects. Therefore the enterprise data architecture function needs to be able to multiply itself, and to communicate effectively to the rest of the organisation to ensure it makes the greatest impact. It needs to:

- Build relationships. The Enterprise Data Architect needs to influence people across the organisation. As such much of the day-to-day work may include getting-to-know-you meetings, how-can-we-help? meetings, and understanding current issues, but also socialising ideas, gaining feedback and promoting understanding. This work can often be evangelical in nature, as the data architect needs to be able to actively promote the benefits of data architecture, accepted best practice techniques, standards and tools to other areas of the organisation and external suppliers where necessary. Key areas include:
    - Engineering teams
    - Project managers
    - Chief Data Officer (CDO)
    - Chief Control Officer (CCO)
    - Chief Executive Officer (CEO)
    - Chief Risk Officer (CRO)
    - Chief Operating Officer (COO)
    - Other architecture leads
    - Business leaders
    - Solution architects

- Run community meetings: Meetings to build community. These may be meetings of data architects, or of the wider data community. These help the (generally small) Enterprise Data Architecture team by disseminating a lot of information widely. They also enable communication, and dispel rumour. Information can flow both from the community to the Enterprise Architecture team and also vice versa.

- Training and mentoring. Design training plans for less experienced data architects. This may well extend to writing the training material itself, in combination with industry training or external training providers. Training also needs to be provided to non-data specialists such as solution architects. The enterprise architect need to assess the training need and tailor the training to be time-effective. In addition the enterprise architect needs to mentor and coach less experienced members of staff and promote an understanding of the value of data architecture and of use of technologies and standards in their domain across IT. This is often one of the most rewarding aspects of the job.

Summary

In this chapter I have looked to describe the discipline and role of enterprise data architecture. This has included:

- Where the Enterprise Data Architect sits in relation to other professionals, and who they may report to.
- What the discipline and role involves. I have divided the enterprise data architecture capabilities into:
    - Future Focus that looks to define where the organisation is going.
    - Current Focus that looks to guide the change that is occurring now.
- I have within each area covered the day to day tasks that the Enterprise Data Architect may cover, and the deliverables they would be expected to create.

I hope that this chapter has given the reader a comprehensive understanding of the discipline and role of an Enterprise Data Architect.

Chapter 7: Project Data Architecture

Introduction

So, after having had a look at Enterprise Data Architecture, we can now have a look at Project Data Architecture.

Project Data Architecture is data architecture at the micro level, operating where development happens, and databases are created. It is generally more technical, and it has a more direct relationship with delivering value to the customer or the organisation. It is generally aligned with the Information Technology (IT) part of the organisation.

The primary role of the Project Data Architect is to create the project data design, and to manage this design through the many stages to delivery.

Position and Reporting Lines

The Project Data Architect can be positioned in the organisation in a number of ways. Most common is either :

- If working in a large project - reporting to the project manager within a larger project. The Project Data Architect would be at a similar level to other roles such as Business Analyst, Solution Architect and similar.
- If working on smaller projects: reporting to a larger data architecture function, in which case the Project Data Architect is not dedicated to a single project but may have a small portfolio of projects and they share their time across them.
- Other options include reporting to a senior Solution Architect in large projects alongside other specialists such as an Infrastructure Architect or Security Architect.

What is Project Data Architecture?

The discipline of Project Data Architecture exists to ensure that an individual project meets data architecture requirements. This is focus on the small scale, an individual element of functionality or collection of such elements. A bounded group within which the project has control.

The discipline has a focus on key outcomes. First the design needs to meet the requirements of the business. The business is giving money to IT to meet its requirements. However these need to be balanced with the responsibility of the project to the organisation. These cover the risk of delivery and the requirement to be a good corporate citizen.

So a good data design:

- Maximises re-useability
- Minimises technical debt
- Is consistent with the data strategy
- Minimises duplication
- Minimises data risk
- Maximises consistency

As said the project data architect tries to balance the requirements of the business, the standards and best practices of the organisation. It is often not an easy balancing act to achieve well, as in the conflict between "quick" and "cheap" and "good", it is the former two that often win in modern business environments.

In this chapter I will go through the key responsibilities and stages in creating a good data design, and then look at the many wider responsibilities of the Project Data Architect.

Project Design

In this section I will cover the key stages in data design. I will cover the Project Data Architect's role and why it is so important.

Understanding the Problem

The first step for the Project Data Architect is to understand the problem the project is looking to solve. This involves a number of key activities:

- Understanding the project from a business context, identification of the **business aims** the project is looking to achieve and identification of the data impacts of these aims. This will include understanding the data that is supporting the business process to be created and/or modified.

- Liaison with key business and IT stakeholders to understand the **data requirements** of the project and the potential data solutions. Documentation of the detailed data requirements, including existing data elements, and new elements to be created.

However, as mentioned above, there is likely to be pressure for a "quick" and "cheap" solution in most business environments. So from the outset the project data architect needs to understand and prepare for this pressure.

A key part of the role is articulation of key data concepts to business and IT stakeholders. The Data Architect needs to be an evangelist for data within the project and the wider organisation, able to balance the needs of the project and IT to develop a solution that delivers for data. Thus the Data Architect needs to explain key data issues that will come up during the project lifecycle.

The architect needs to expect pushback against a detailed consideration of data issues. Data discipline has not traditionally been at the forefront of solution design, so this will be a "hearts and minds" exercise to ensure that all project developers, stakeholders managers and architects are on the same page.

Creation of Data Requirements

After understanding the requirements, they need to be documented. In order to design a solution, you need to define what it will do. These are requirements, and yes, they apply just as much - if not more - in the agile or devops world as in the old waterfall world. "Make it up as you go along" is not, and never has been, a way of creating good design.

Without requirements, the most likely outcome is bad design. So what do good data requirements look like? Well they need to consider the data within a project from a variety of angles:

- Data Modelling
- Data Quality
- Data Volume
- Data Sensitivity
- Data Types and Formats
- Data Integrity
- Data Storage and its efficiency
- Data Extraction and Use

In short, all of the aspects of data covered by the scope. As a result of this consideration the design should be better, and more likely to meet requirements, which means a happier customer and a smoother build.

It is also noted that detailed documentation of requirements is a protection mechanism for the architect. Clearly stating what the requirements of the business are, and agreeing them with the business, protects the architect and the project from awkward conversations later.

In almost every area of human experience things go easier and quicker with a plan. I am consistently surprised that in data a very common approach is "make it up as you go along."

Creating a Design

Once requirements are defined, the next stage is creating a design. This is the key deliverable for the Project Data Architect, who will draw on all their experience to make the best design for the requirements in question. It is difficult to write down everything involved, but key tasks will include:

- Understanding of the potential options for delivery of the data design, including pre-existing solutions that may exist. This involves a thorough knowledge of the data estate, reaching out to Enterprise Data Architecture and potentially Global Data Architecture.

- It may also include discussion and iteration of the potential designs with the solution architect, business stakeholders, and developers.

- Ensuring any design complies with strategic direction. This is inherent in the design phase, however any exceptions to strategic direction will need to be taken through the appropriate design council.

- Understanding that if strategic development is not possible, that technical debt must be minimised and a clear path to strategic state identified. This may involve developing not just the solution design, but transition states and end states.

- Compliance with organisational standards for data architecture.

- Compliance with tooling standards. Many organisations have standard products for standard use cases (e.g. ETL, data storage). A project cannot simply choose a product and implement. Any new tooling may need to be taken through approval authorities. If new data tooling is required, the Project Data Architect needs to take the project through appropriate approval forums.

- Meeting current legal and regulatory requirements within the scope. The Data Architect needs to understand legal frameworks such as GDPR, data sharing, outsourcing, etc. The Project Data Architect needs to document how these legal regulations are met.

- Understanding of data quality needs, and how they will be implemented within the project. This includes the way in which the project will ensure data integrity so that data is transmitted without any loss in quality, and also the consideration of how the quality requirements of the end user are met and demonstrated.

- Identification and separation of data flows within the project. This will include developing and creating a data flow diagram and/or sequence diagram in conjunction with the solution architect.

- The creation of a project data model that both meets business needs and is also in alignment with standards for data modelling.

- Development and approval of new data patterns, if required, and take such patterns through appropriate forums.

- Liaising with the solution architect to develop the overall detailed project design for data.

- Management of data-related approvals. Many organisations will have approval cycles for project designs. As the owner of the data design it is the Project Data Architect's responsibility to navigate the approval cycle.

- Making sure the design meets business requirements, both functional and non-functional. This includes:
  - Design of the testing for data
  - Mapping the testing to requirements
  - Understanding of testing methodologies
  - Integration of data within those methodologies
  - Creation of test scenarios

- Liaison with the Chief Data Office and developers throughout the project lifecycle.

- Working with development teams to guide them on the appropriate implementation of data related technologies.

Project Architect Deliverables

So, to make this more real, what should the Project Data Architect create during the project? Key deliverables are listed below. Some of these may be joint deliverables with the solution architect, and in these cases it is the data aspect of these deliverables that will, obviously, be the data architect's concern.

- Documentation of data scope. What data is within the scope of the project? Initially this can be as high level as "claims data for the UK" or "mortgage application data for the UK." As the project progresses a more detailed description of the scope should evolve, to the point where individual data fields are described.

- Data requirements. Traditionally projects are very bad at this, but it is critical. What do the business users actually want to achieve with the data?

- A data flow diagram. A description of what data flows from where to where. Note that this is very different from a solution architecture diagram which typically contains a number of components with arrows between them. This tells the reader nothing about the data flow, it merely states that there **is** a data flow. Nor does "ftp" or similar describe much about a data flow – it just states the technical mechanism that allows it to take place.

- A logical/conceptual data model. All projects should have a data model – a description on how data is structured. I would go further and say the data architect should also describe the reasons behind the data modelling decisions, less someone later feel that they should be changed.

- Database design. This will include the way in which the data is stored (essentially a physical data model), how it will be accessed, how queries run, the design of those queries, why they should be implemented in that way, indexing, which fields are primary keys, etc.

- Documentation of compliance with data legislation. Data legislation is becoming more complex and the penalties for breach more onerous. Data legislation may include, but is not limited to:
    - Data privacy
    - GDPR
    - Outsourcing
    - Data transfer across borders
    - Data quality
    - BCBS239

- Documentation of compliance with the organisation's data strategy. This includes where there are exceptions or divergence, why these decisions have been taken and who has approved this divergence.

- Any documentation of compliance with mandatory organisational polices around data, for example metadata standards.

- (obviously) A data design, high level, medium level and low level, describing how data will be ingested into the project boundary, used within it and then output. This should include all components, and clear documentation should exist on all fields, all transformations, with a description of when and how data will move, what decisions will be made on the data, how its integrity will be assured, how its quality will be assured, and how it will meet the data requirements as previously documented.

- A data-specific test plan and results.

Wider Design Considerations

Whilst all the above is going on, the Project Data Architect needs to have a few other key areas in mind.

Minimise Duplicative Effort

In reality many uses of data within an organisation use the same data. For example, sales data will be used by:

- Sales professionals themselves
- Their managers for reviewing performance
- HR for calculating compensation
- Management for reviewing performance
- Investors looking at company prospects for the future

.... and many others.

This duplication of use applies to most data within any organisation. It is one of the reasons why data quality is so important, as one error has an impact many times.

It is unfortunately common for each use case to extract data separately from the operational systems and hence duplicate data structures. Typical organisations have thousands of point-to-point feeds. Many different solutions are built using the same data, but each solution extracts data from source systems itself, duplicating work many times.

So the project data architect needs to make sure that what they are designing isn't simply a duplication of work another department or project has already delivered.

An ideal solution would be for an organisation-wide solution where data is extracted from source systems once, and then consumed many times. This can save vast amounts of money in duplicative work. However this may need to be implemented centrally.

Minimise Technical Debt

Here, I need to explain what technical debt is. Technical debt is the cost that is incurred by not doing things right first time. If you implement a "quick and dirty" solution today then the debt you incur is the cost of having to do it properly tomorrow.

If data is done badly, it often has to be rectified later – either by another project redoing the original work, or – more likely – by downstream users spending time and effort to rebuild the data they actually want, rather than using what the project has supplied.

Sometimes clever design means a short-cut solution can be avoided, or that technical debt can be minimised by designing a solution that isn't totally throw-away, but can provide a stepping stone to get to a strategic solution.

So the Project Data Architect needs to look to minimise technical debt. They needs to make sure that if compromises are made from a "good" solution, that such compromises can be reversed easily later. Being clever about data up front means less work later.

Facilitate Data Access

All data collected is vital to the organisation because it either provides a picture of the customer or the workings of the organisation, both of which are critical to success. Any Project Data Architect, understanding data flow, will know this.

A common problem in many organisations is sourcing data and bringing it together into a single location for measurement and analytics. However, due to the focus on functional implementation, in most organisations data is locked in functional silos – the contact data is in the Customer Relationship Management System (CRMS), the product data is in the product system, and customer preferences are locked in a silo attached to the application for which the preference applies.

None of this is ideal and to have a true picture of the organisation requires access to its data. This is often described as a "360 Degree View."

Good data architecture maximises the ability to re-use data. The Project Data Architect should design solutions that enable easy access to data.

Ensure Data Consistency

One of the key roles of a Project Data Architect is to ensure data consistency. I will divide consistency into two areas. Consistency between systems and consistency within a system.

Consistency between systems is a common problem in organisations. The common example is that finance run a report of a division's performance and it does not match the same report on theoretically the same data run by the division themselves.

The problem is poor curation of data flow. In this case the design of one system has modified the data. This has either been by dropping data - a data integrity problem, or actual corruption. The data finance is using, and the data the division is using, are not consistent. This is a "consistency between systems" problem.

By designing the flow of data appropriately the data architect can ensure a single source of truth for information.

The second area is "consistency within a system." Here the system needs to conform to a data model, and it is part of the project data architect's job to ensure this is the case. So within an individual system, we should not have different addresses for a customer, and the customer name should be the same on the order as on the invoice, and dates should all have the same format.

Key Benefits

I'd like to re-iterate in more detail here the benefits a Project Data Architect brings to a project. Key benefits that a Project Data Architect brings are:

Minimise Cost
Without a data architect, solutions are not designed by specialists in the area.

So they make mistakes - this is understandable, they are not specialists. We have all been in situations where, when approaching a problem for the first time, we get half-way through and realise the solution would have been much better - and cheaper - if we'd taken a different path.

Using a specialist means data is implemented in the right way. A common example is data migrations. Any data architect will tell you most older source systems contain a lot of "rough" data. If a data transfer from an old system to a new system is attempted without understanding and accounting for this data - whether by remediating it, excluding it, or whatever solution is taken - then the data migration will fail and the project team will need to try this all again. This is very expensive, and what applies for data migration applies elsewhere too.

Anecdote

In one data migration the initial attempt at migration into the new system failed when less than 5% of the data tables transferred. Everything had to be done again.

So, if you have a data architect on board, your project will go more smoothly, be less frustrating, and cost less.

Matching data modelling to the business use
Modelling is very linked to data design. When business systems are designed the data structure should be matched to business use. If this is not the case then there will be a direct impact on the business ability to use the system.

I'm aware this may be a difficult concept to grasp, so the easiest way to demonstrate this is with an example:

An insurance company once had a category within its database for "electric vehicles." Initially, there were very few vehicles in this category - electric milk floats were about the only example. All the vehicles in that category were assumed to have a similar risk. This category had a very low insurance risk. Insurance premiums were priced per category.

However with the rise of electric vehicles, especially very fast electric sports cars - this no longer met business needs. Either the premiums for milk floats would be too high, or the premium for electric sports cars would be too low.

In this instance the data structure did not allow the organisation to price its product appropriately. It would be losing money as a result.

So the way data is structured must match with its use. The data architect needs to design the structure of the data so that it meets organisational needs.

I would add there is, of course, a way around the problem above. It is possible to design very complex queries to extract certain car makes and models from the database and price accordingly. However this is difficult and error-prone, and may require changes to business processes. For example, drop-down lists in front end systems may require rewriting, and training given to ensure that right cars are put in the right categories.

Not thinking about the data model can have significant consequences. This example also demonstrates the way that systems can change over time to be unsuitable for business use as the world changes.

Optimising data performance
One of the most important reasons for the data architect's presence on a project is to optimise data performance. It is common in the absence of a data architect for data structures to be built in the easiest and quickest possible way. This may not be the best way to meet requirements.

Developers are commonly not data experts, and are often pressurised by a project manager to deliver as fast as possible. Developers are also not end users, and are unlikely to directly feel the impact if it turns out the system is unusable. Therefore a data structure that is quick and easy to implement is likely to win over a data structure that is harder to implement but gives better performance.

Incorrect structures will result in poor performance or, worse, a user finding it impossible to do what they want with the data. The data structure for writing to a database is **not** the data structure for reading a report. An organisation needs a data architect to design data structures that will meet the business needs.

Summary

In this chapter I have looked to describe the discipline and role of Project Data Architecture.

I have explained that the main role of a Project Data Architect is to create the data design and manage the delivery of that design - not as a project manager, but being on-hand as the data subject matter expert, and ensure the project implements the data design right.

I have explained that the Project Data Architect needs to have two hats, one looking inward at the project itself, and the other looking outward, doing the right thing for the organisation. Balancing these is a challenge.

I have also briefly summarised the value of the discipline to both the organisation and the project, and why the Project Data Architect is critical to project success.

Chapter 8: Governing Data Architecture

Introduction

Finally within this section of the book I would like to cover the governance of data architecture. This is something that sits very firmly within the "enterprise" section of the discipline, but deserves its own chapter.

There is no one-size-fits-all answer as to how to govern Data Architecture. What works depends on the structure and culture of the organisation. I have covered in this chapter a number of industry approaches, and I've also covered my impressions of how the various techniques work. Such impressions are clearly subjective and limited to the organisations with which I have had experience, so should not be regarded as gospel. If I say a certain approach is more effective, then this is clearly only in my own experience.

Approaches to Data Architecture governance vary widely. Some organisations very much focus on a "command and control" approach to architecture governance, others on a "hygiene" approach, others on an approach of exception reporting. In my view the best approach is a blended approach, which covers the problem from a number of angles. Specifically;

- Hygiene for the Organisation
- Design Guidance
- Specific to the Project
- Data Controls and Evidencing
- Exception reporting

The first two are put in place before a change is attempted, the third whilst a change is underway, and the last two after a change has occurred. Together I feel this enables a holistic and effective approach to governance.

Hygiene

Data Literacy

It is much, much easier to stop problems occurring in the first place rather than having to clean them up later, or, worse, having to live with the consequences. However a Data Architecture function often has limited resources. Critical to turning an impossible job into a manageable one is recruiting as many people to help as possible. Ideally, everyone.

Improving data literacy in the organisation is one of the most important changes an enterprise architect can make. The theory is data across the organisation can be improved if everyone knows the behaviours that are acceptable and best practice.

If everyone involved in creating data structures is aware of the right thing to do – and, importantly, **why** it is the right thing to do, then many problems don't occur.

In addition, improving data literacy is self-multiplying. A data literate individual will change the wrong thing if they see it - if you have the right culture.

Training

Creating data literacy is challenging. Key is training. This can come from a number of sources.

- Mandatory training. Most large organisations have mandatory training required every year. Rolling data training into this is one way of raising awareness, but this kind of training has limited penetration. Most staff will move through mandatory training as quickly as possible, the objective to finish the training, not learn anything. Therefore other approaches are needed as well.

- Presentations. Typically the approach is a senior individual – potentially the Enterprise Data Architect – presenting to smaller groups of people. Effectiveness is much better than the mandatory training, however this depends on the presentation, which **must** be tailored to the audience. A technical presentation to execs will not be received well, and in fact can seriously damage credibility. A high level presentation to developers will leave them wondering when you are going to get to the interesting bit. It is worth noting language. Data specialists have a danger of disappearing into a language of their own, and you have to be very careful to avoid "data-speak."

- **Micro-courses.** Shorter courses easier to fit into the working day but provide a degree of isolation from the working environment. These would typically be run by either a third party or by a senior individual within the organization. The problem with the latter is knowing about a subject does not necessarily mean that you are good at explaining it to others. The advantage of this approach is that – especially with smaller groups – focus is better, and the cost is significantly lower than fully external courses.

- **Peer training/champions.** Training one person in each area of the organization at quite a detailed level who can then be champions for their area. Whilst good in theory this only works if others actually ask them about data. If others simply carry on doing what they were always doing then it doesn't solve the problem.

- **External Training:** External training tends to be very effective, as you are taking the individual out of the distracting environment of the working day. Concentration is a lot better, and the likelihood of retaining knowledge is a lot better too. However – as always – this is critically dependent on the quality of the training material, and unfortunately this is often not pitched at the right level for the participants, not engaging enough, or tries to cover too much ground in not enough time. Of course the main challenge with this kind of course is getting people out of the work environment, and of course resultant cost.

So, what is the right training approach? My view would be "do everything you can." Or, to put it another way, a blended approach. The typical approach would be to divide the organisation into blocks of people with similar characteristics and develop a training plan to use the most effective method for each group.

Culture

One of the most difficult things to do within an organisation is to change culture. In respect of data, there are two things you are looking to change:

- Data literacy
- Data confidence

I have covered data literacy above, Data confidence is the knowledge that raising data issues is the right thing to do, and knowing the right way of doing it, and having processes in place to enable it.

If an employee notices a data quality issue then they not only need to know what to do, how to escalate it, and that the escalation will be appreciated and won't get them into trouble, but they also need to be able to see results. Employees who raise concerns and then don't see their concerns addressed will rapidly stop raising them.

Data confidence is something that has to be led from the top. It has to be a message that is repeated, and lived by. Data leaders need to be examples of good behaviour, and be responsive to concerns raised.

Design Guidance

The next area of governance is also based around stopping the problem occurring in the first place. However it is more specific than the hygiene factors mentioned above. This is design guidance, that can be used by individual change projects so they know the right thing to do.

Reference Architecture and Patterns

The central team create a set of design guidelines which explain the design principles that need to be followed by the organisation. These guidelines can be updated by the submission of patterns to a team for approval and hence the overall design guidelines grow.

The way this works is that a high level reference architecture is created. This is an end to end design that explains the overall target architecture across the organisation. It will explain the overall building blocks and how they fit together.

Next down in detail is the patterns. These are subsets of the overall reference architecture and – for an element – go into detail. They would normally expected to include detailed information on the architecture, the data flows, their contents, and how the data should flow.

The patterns give the projects real practical help and guidance on detailed implementation patterns. It is common for new patterns to be approved at a forum specific to that purpose. Hence the overall pattern library evolves and new patterns can be re-used by others. It is also common for projects following an established, approved pattern to have lighter-touch governance than a project outside the patterns.

Tooling Approvals and Forums

Tooling approval forums approve tools for use cases across the organisation. At any one time, in any organisation, there will be:

- Tools that are considered legacy or being demised.
- Tools that are used throughout the organisation.
- Tools that are niche.
- Tools that are under consideration, pilot or "Proof-of-Concept."
- Tools that are barred.

Most organisations – especially larger ones – are bombarded by vendors looking for sales. Unless there is clear governance the organisation will end up using many tools for the same use case, paying a fortune in license fees, and being unable to share knowledge across the organisation as different parts of the organisation are using different tooling.

A clear governance process, where tools are approved for specific uses, significantly reduces this risk.

Global Data Model

A global data model enables an organisation to have a consistent data structure and consistent data meaning across all of its data. This is important and valuable.

Consider the problem: System A holds data on customers but has three fields – firstname, middlename, surname. System B holds data on customers but has two fields, firstnames, surname. It is now almost impossible to match customers, unless complicated queries are written looking for the space between first and middle names in the second system, splitting the data, and then matching to the three fields of the first system. What a lot of work! Wouldn't it be easier if all the organisations systems held data in the same format? Worse, the names problem is quite a simple one to solve. In many instances it is actually impossible to translate one data model to another.

The second area of this is data definitions. What is a firstname? Given name, family name? Nickname? Easy in the UK, this becomes more problematic in other areas of the world, notably Asia. Equally what is an address, how is it formatted? Even within the UK there are significant differences between the way addresses are formatted (e.g. flats in Scotland). If it is not written down then each implementation, each project, each system, will use their own guess at what is right.

The creation and maintenance and, importantly, enforcement of a data model is a major help to overall design, and preventing issues occurring in the long term.

Specific to the Project

As well as factors that apply to the whole organisation, there are also governance mechanisms that apply at a project level. The advantage here is that each governance mechanism can be tailored to the level of governance appropriate to the project. Such mechanisms are listed below.

Gateway

The most simple – and sadly most effective – way of governing data architecture is to have a gateway process with signoffs. A design will be submitted by the project to an architecture governing body, which will signoff that the project is obtaining the data from the right place, using appropriate tooling, using appropriate architecture patterns, data structures, modelling standards and the like. This also allows the senior architects to review for more esoteric issues that the project may not have thought of, such as ethics, legal and regulatory issues.

The problem with this approach is that it is clunky, and uses a lot of senior time, and delays projects that may need to return to the governing forum many times to get approval. Slots on the forum's agenda may not be instantly available. As a result many months can be lost.

This process also does not work well with agile development. When development is proceeding in two week sprints there is no time for repeated signoff meetings. The best that can be done is an overall assessment of the project, but then this doesn't account for the changes that will occur during agile – or devops – development.

Multiple Gateways.

Possibly even worse – but extremely common - is a multiple gateway scenario where there may be a gateway at an early design stage, another when the design is formalised, another before build and another before go-live. This does minimise risk of solutions being built inappropriately but is very onerous on the project. It also uses a vast amount of senior review time. Delivery is slow, and this level of supervision is simply not necessary for the vast majority of projects.

Again, this doesn't work for agile or devops projects.

Consultancy Model (Subject Matter Expert)

In this model the architecture practice employs a number of data architects who act as subject matter experts (SME) for the areas of change (typically projects). Projects would come to the SMEs at multiple stages of the project lifecycle for advice. It is a little akin to the multiple gateways approach above however as the SME is only one person – as opposed to a forum – the approach is flexible and faster.

Embedded Expert

In this approach each project includes an embedded expert (i.e. a data architect) who understands the appropriate designs and can advise the project on appropriate solutions.

The disadvantages of this solution are that is it expensive to have an embedded expert, so only very large projects can choose this path. On the other hand, large projects often do have dedicated data architects, and certainly when the budget can stand it, it is a good solution.

Design Peer Reviews

The design for the project is put through a peer review. This has the advantage that the peers are usually easier to get hold of than senior SMEs, and it performs an effective review. Having to justify and present design decisions to your peers is often a good way of exploring any weaknesses.

The drawback is that peer reviews can become an echo chamber where poor practice is accepted because the data and design literacy of the peer group is poor.

Data Controls and Evidencing

Another common control method for architecture is documentation. Each change project needs to complete a number of steps and document these steps before they can go live.

The kind of documents that can be included are:
- Documents showing data context and data flows.
- Data requirements documentation.
- Documents showing how the data design meets requirements (traceability).
- Data security assessments and design.
- Data sourcing design.
- Proof of uploading details to enterprise repositories.
- Proof of gateway approvals.
- Documents showing how data quality or integrity are ensured.
- Documents showing how legal and regulatory requirements are met.
- Documentation of the considerations around data privacy.
- Documentation of how he design meets architectural standards.

The list here can be endless and in many organisations often is. The challenge is that projects feel that they are drowning in red tape, agility is compromised, and delivery is delayed.

Exception Reporting

Of course, all of the above – to a certain extent, rely on trust. We trust that what is actually built will reflect what has been agreed in reviews, and we trust that developers will do the right thing because they are data literate and know what not to do. However projects are often under tight delivery deadlines, and there is a strong incentive to cut corners. So, how does an organisation find out – after the fact – that architectural governance has been followed? This has been a problem for many years in most organisations.

A more recent development is the process of automating architecture control. This has come about through automated tools that exist on public cloud providers, and also the greater capability of analytics.

Appropriate Sourcing

There are two pre-requisites for this automated control but it's a good one.

If an organisation has (1) a list of appropriate sources for data sets (so, for example, that customer data must come from the CRM system in the UK) and (2) also has a list of all applications and their interfaces that is updated as new interfaces are created, it is possible to automatically check whether the correct data is being sourced from the correct place and flag where this is not the case.

Obviously the effectiveness of this control will depend on whether new interfaces are added to the registry, and it also has a drawback that poor sources – for example spreadsheets – are unlikely to "officially exist" in an enterprise registry, but even so, this approach can be very useful.

Design Documents

If every project creates a design document as discussed above, and all the design documents are the same standard format, then it is possible to automatically scan the design document for effective architectural design.

So, for example, if a design document states the data sources a project is using, then there can be a check back against the "list of golden sources" to ensure that the appropriate sources are being used.

If the design document contains details of the data elements being created or used, then it is possible to scan to see whether personally identifiable information is being created or used. The scope of this control is only really limited by the size and complexity of the design document. However organisations should shy away from creating an overly complex document as it may be difficult to get projects to complete it.

Automatic Lineage

Data lineage is a hot topic at present, and many organisations struggle with understanding where their data is flowing, from where to where. It is possible to automate this process to an extent, however care should be taken.

Traditional means of documentation of lineage is to use very manual tools. The problem with this approach is that it takes time, and as soon as any changes occur then it is instantly out of date. This has not stopped many organisations wasting vast amounts of resources on such tasks.

This is one area where tools can help considerably. Tools exist on the market that will read in metadata from ETL programmes and create lineage diagrams with no human intervention. This can save considerable time.

However, whilst the tooling is typically very good at reading ETL data from the same vendor, it has variable results in reading ETL from other vendors or competitors.

Monitoring Development

Many organisations have a system which is used by developers for recording progress with development. This is generally issue tracking software and/or project management software.

It is possible to automatically review this software to highlight areas where there may be architectural issues. So, for example, if a project is mentioning the words "date of birth" then it is highly likely that it is dealing with customer data. Therefore this can be used to highlight to the legal team who can interface with the project and ensure that GDPR regulation is being followed.

- The advantage of this is that it can detect issues whilst the project is in-flight.
- The disadvantage is that once projects know that their development is being monitored they will avoid using the development system or being very careful on what is being placed there, in which case the organisation is back to square one.

Graph mapping
If the data is available, a very effective way of monitoring architecture is mapping sources and data flows in a graph database. Humans react a lot better to visual aids and a picture of the architecture is easy to interpret.

You may feel that I am simply describing a solution diagram, but not quite. Consider if we can view the entire organisation as a unit. We can not only see what data is flowing from one solution to another, but second order and third order connections.

This enables us to identify architectural risk. Consider, for example, a business critical system that is highly resilient. Its upstream data feeds may also be highly resilient. However upstream of that again, what is the situation? The business critical system may never actually fall over but may contain no data because upstream data provision is not built to the same level of resiliency.

Looking at architectural risk as a holistic approach is very new, but is also essential for the larger organisation. It brings a much better understanding of the risk to the organisation than looking at projects or systems in silos.

Cloud providers
The rise of cloud providers has enabled a significant change in the ability of organisations to monitor their architecture. Since all cloud architecture is essentially just data points in the cloud provider's inventory, seeing what data is being transferred from where to where is relatively easy.

In this case an organisation can see exactly what has been built and where and what it connects to.

More than this, most cloud providers provide data scanning tools to identify the types of data that are being transferred and stored, automatically detecting sensitive data such as credit card numbers or personally identifiable data such as customer names.

Furthermore, given that many cloud vendors allow very close monitoring of the spend in any of their projects, it is possible to monitor the storage used and also to monitor the storage increase over time. So, for example, if there is a big jump in storage used, then this can be automatically flagged for review. This can also help with tooling. It is possible to create automatic reports on the tooling that is being used on cloud. This can be mapped to the organisations tooling strategy and tooling permissions

In addition, the organization can see the patterns that have been used to build on cloud and can match them to the approved patters in the organization.

Lastly many cloud providers can supply a lineage tool that is native to their products and allows clear discovery, mapping and visualization of the detailed data flows.

When building it cloud it is possible to have a close and effective control of architecture, as it is built.

Summary

In this chapter I have looked at the various ways architecture can be governed. Governance splits into:

- Hygiene for the Organisation
- Design Guidance
- Specific to the Project
- Data Controls and Evidencing
- Exception reporting

There is no one-size-fits all for architectural governance, and what is actually effective will depend on the organisation's culture, the way its projects are managed, what tooling is used by development teams, and many other factors.

However, governance is essential. If an organisation is looking to manage and improve its data architecture then it needs to know what is being built is consistent with strategy. Without knowing this it is not in control.

SECTION 2: Building Blocks

- What are the basic building blocks?

- A deep dive into all the architectural building blocks in more detail.

  - Databases
  - Data in Motion
  - Reporting and Visualisation
  - Cloud
  - Data Ecosystems
  - Third Parties

- Data Modelling

Chapter 9: Section Introduction

Although I touched on this earlier in the book, a key part of data architecture is understanding the technical building blocks with which architects work, how they fit together, and what are the advantages – and disadvantages - of each type of building block.

In this section of the book I will describe the basic building blocks with which all data architects work. We will cover these building blocks in the direction of data flow, so running from the initial touch points where data enters the organisation's systems, and finishing where the data is used for reporting to management or a regulator.

In general data flows from high granularity to low granularity, being aggregated at each stage of the data flow. The data that is entered by a customer or is created when a customer buys an item is very granular. This granular level of detail (for example, that £1 was spent on some nails at a hardware shop) is not really much use to anyone further down the data flow. The people further down the flow may want to know how much has been spent on nails in a day (for re-ordering stock) or in a store (store performance) or how much a customer has bought in total (customer relationship management) but all this is aggregated data. The only place the granular detail is needed is the transaction itself.

Also in general data flows from an immediate timescale to a less immediate one. The transaction is in the instant, however reporting (on stock, the customer or the branch) does not need to happen instantly. In fact saying that the branch has just sold £1 of nails a second ago is meaningless. It is the aggregated amount over time (say, in a day) that is useful. Mostly it is both unnecessary – and ridiculously expensive – to keep "instant" time throughout the organisation.

Lastly, data generally flows from critical systems to less critical systems. The point of sale terminal must work, otherwise the customer cannot buy anything. If no customers can buy anything the business cannot survive. However if the CEO doesn't get his daily report then he will be annoyed and heads may roll, but the business will survive.

This second section of the book starts with a short overview of all systems (the "basic building blocks"). It is not necessary for the data architect to know all of these in detail to the level that would be required as a developer or system designer, but knowing what they are and what they do is essential.

Deep Dive

I will then perform a deep dive into a number of areas where the Data Architect very much does need to know the detail – and will be expected to do so in a working environment. I will cover:

- Databases
- Data in Motion
- Reporting and Visualisation
- Cloud
- Data Ecosystems
- Third Party Data
- Data Modelling

At the end of this section the reader should know both what data architecture is and the role of a Data Architect (from Section 1) and the components in play that make up data architectures (from Section 2). This sets the stage for Section 3 of the book which explains common data architectures in organisations, common pain points, and how to solve them.

Chapter 10: Basic Building Blocks

Introduction

In the first chapter in this section, I'll go through data architecture building blocks. The objective is to familiarise the reader with the various components that comprise data architectures at a high level. I'll largely follow the classic data flow from the initial touch points where data enters an organisation though aggregation points through to data consumption.

The broad brush areas covered are:

- Channels
- Core Systems
- Databases (i.e. data aggregation and storage)
- Data Consumption (reporting and analysis)

Channels

Channels are the point at which data enters an organisation. Historically they started as being just branch, and then expanded in turn into phone, web, and mobile in the 1990s. I'll cover these in that sequence.

Branch

By a "branch" I am using this term to represent a local outlet of the organisation in question. So a branch of a bank, a retail outlet that is one store of a national chain, or similar. The most traditional of the channels, this needs little explaining. Although branches have been in existence since the start of commerce, there have been many changes with the advent of computers.

Typically now branch staff have limited functionality available to them and connectivity is limited to relatively simple terminals that connect back to core systems housed in a data centre. Branches are therefore limited to basic transactions or transactions that have to have a face to face component – for example where copies of original documentation is required or goods are physically exchanged.

Phone

Another traditional channel, but whereas the customer used to ring a branch, now there are dedicated call centres. Call centres tend to have a greater range of options available to them and access to more systems, as being located on-site it is easy to connect staff to the disparate systems that make up the organisation's data landscape.

From a data point of view call centre systems are often extremely complex. Not only will they route and record calls, measure staff performance, they will also often use scripts to guide staff on answering queries and contain facilities for managers to listen in to calls.

Call centres are much more than simply a lot of people answering phones. From an IT point of view they are often powerhouses of information, and are probably the most complex channel.

Web and Mobile

Web
With the explosion of the Internet in the 1990s the Internet became one of the main ways in which customers communicated with organisations. This was a revolution. It became possible for customers to visit a website, order goods and services, which would then be passed to a fulfillment system with no manual input. Rather than visiting a branch or ringing a call centre, the whole process was automated.

This represented a massive change in the way companies did business. It also introduced fundamental changes in the way that IT systems worked. Now, there was a website, there were online customers who had accounts, there were hooks back into source systems which had to be strictly controlled and all of this could happen out of sight.

So not only was there the means to process information, there was a need to manage that information. Fortunately, one of the things computers are very good at is collating, storing and managing information.

Mobile

The last revolution was more of an evolution. With the advent of smartphones, rather than customers interacting with a customer from their PC, the customer was carrying a PC around with them.

The big data difference from a mobile point of view was the interface. A mobile phone was a very different interface from a PC, and many companies struggled to create an interface that worked for the customer.

Third parties

Lastly, it is worth mentioning another area of complexity, data that originates from third parties. Many organisations share data with, and receive data from, other organisations. This data may be incoming credit reports, it may be a regulator, it may be a supplier. It may also be a third party selling your goods on your behalf, or a comparison aggregator.

Integrating third party information into core systems remains a challenge to this day. One of the main challenges is data quality – how do you ensure that the data that is being received is correct? Other challenges include where to store the data, how to ensure integrity, and, of course, security – you are, by necessity, allowing a third party to send data into your own systems.

Way of doing this safely exist, a key one being Application Programming Interfaces (APIs), which I will cover later in the book.

Core Systems

After passing through channel interfaces, data flows into core systems. Core systems are the central hub of many organisations. They do the heavy lifting in the company. When computers were first used, one of the first areas to be automated was the basic day to day transactions that are the bread and butter of any company operations.

These core systems – often running on a mainframe - were serviced by green-text terminals to allow user input. Surprisingly, many of these systems still exist.

Although time has moved on – and despite a lot of talk about microservices (of which more later) most companies rely on these core fulfillment systems to perform most day to day processing to serve customers. So, what are they, what are their characteristics, and what to they do?

Monoliths

These are typically large, complex central systems that contain a number of modules which interconnect but are mutually dependent.

They are likely to contain information on customers, orders, balances, potentially stock, transactions – in short everything the business needs to function. They will supply the stock details to the website, they will receive the order from the website, they will record the transaction and adjust the customer account and current balance, process the order, and record the dispatch.

These systems are often proprietary – i.e. created by a third party who specialises in creating software for a particular industry. They are also generally modular, with an orders module, a customer module, a fees and interest module and so on. This is due to the way in which they are developed, with many smaller teams concentrating on specific areas which are integrated at a later point. However all the modules are integrated and importantly mutually dependent. They cannot exist separate to the whole. The ensemble cannot be broken up - hence the use of the term "monolith."

These systems will generally include logging for audit purposes, and may also include other features, such as some form of limited reporting and analytics. These systems are critical to the operation of the organisation.

From a data point of view they will generally include within them significant data stores. These include short term data stores for temporarily holding information, or the longer-term permanent record of transactions. What they will not generally hold is historical data. They are not optimised for bulk data storage, so data is archived from them on a regular basis.

The data model will be optimised for operations, and may be set by the manufacturer and not changeable by the organisation in which they are installed.

Monolith-plus Systems

A second type of core system are "Monolith-Plus" systems. In short, this is a monolith with bolt-ons. It is common. Monoliths by their nature are difficult to modify. Therefore if a new capability comes to the market – the need to process certain types of payments, or the wish to add a product that the existing monolith doesn't quite cope with, then it may be easier in the short run to create a bolt-on to the monolith.

This can get out of hand, with many bolt-ons being created to cope with successive changes, so the "core system" resembles a house where there are more extensions than original property.

These systems become increasingly difficult to change. The organisation becomes increasingly inflexible and the construct becomes more and more unwieldy. At some point large investment will be required to disentangle and rebuild, but that takes political will and deep pockets.

However this is a very common architecture existing in hundreds of thousands of organisations worldwide.

Hub and Spoke

A third type of core system arrangement is the hub-and spoke system. This is where certain common functions – for example customer data – are held in a hub and other systems share that common data between them. This is a more modern architecture, and occurs when organisations start to move towards a customer-centric approach to business.

The evolution of customer centricity.
Its worth spending a moment talking about customer centricity. Back in the olden days, when computers were young, what mattered was the account. Everything was arranged by account number. Customers were merely "attached to" the account. This was all very well, but it meant that if a customer had two accounts, or two products, then the customer name, address, and all other details, would be recorded twice, once against one account and once against another. It also means that if an organisation wanted to have a view of all their interactions with a particular customer, then they couldn't without a lot of analytics.

However, account-centricity was the norm for most of the 80s and 90s. Then customer-centricity became more important. The world was moving and organisations wanted that "360 degree view", seeing all their interactions with the customer in one place. This drives another type of architecture, where customer information was pulled out of monolithic systems – often at great expense, and placed in its own data store. All the product systems then referenced the one place. This is the hub and spoke model.

Where this falls down is there are often many other personal interactions which are still held elsewhere. For example, if we define a customer as someone who bought a product, how do we define those who have not bought anything? This may include people who have applied for a product but not bought it, or people the organisation interacts with but as yet no goods have exchanged hands. From a data point of view they look exactly like customers – so why not treat them like customers?

So the next stage – not yet common – is where all interactions with customers, potential customers or connected parties (for example those holding power-of-attorney) are held in once place. This allows a better understanding of "those with whom the organisation interacts" and also allows the organisation to better understand the linkages between all individuals with whom they deal.

In addition, it allows better data management, de-duplication of individuals, fraud management and adherence with legal restrictions around personal data. Most laws don't separate customers and non-customers – they just state "individuals."

So data constructs are still evolving........

Microservices

Microservice architectures are a modern concept and look to solve the traditional problem with large, single systems. These are true modular systems.

The concept of microservices splits the large monolith up into many separate systems, each performing a tiny part of the overall operation. The idea is to allow flexibility and agility. Key to microservice architectures is minimal connectivity and maximum independence between the modular components. This allows a single microservice to be upgraded if there is an issue without affecting the rest of the system. It also allows the microservice to be duplicated to process a single service in parallel if there is a capacity problem.

There are however drawbacks. Consideration of data is key. Because data flows through all the microservices, changes to data will impact all downstream users of that data. The solution is generally either to federate the ownership of the data – so each microservice has authority over a tiny bit of the overall data set and that authority does not conflict elsewhere – or to have an agreed global data model that everyone agrees with and works to.

This requires care, and many implementers of microservices find it a lot more difficult than initially anticipated. It is easy to re-build an interdependent monolith by mistake despite best intentions.

Databases

After core systems, the next area to cover is databases. I will go into databases in a lot more detail later in its own chapter, but here I want to give an overview of the types of job that databases do. Realistically databases are part of the core competency of the data architect, so this book will cover them in detail.

At its most basic, databases are "a store for data." However the reasons for the storage, the way and which data is stored, the types of data stored and where in the information flow it is stored vary widely.

Back-end Databases

I will start with "back-end databases." These are the data storage device for front end channels. Traditionally the front end channel stored data in a core system. However as more channels were added (branch, call centre, web and mobile users) more systems interacted with core systems.

This became complex and unwieldy. One of the critical problems to solve was what happened if you needed to store data that was only used for one channel. For example, the web login details. In this case it made sense to store this data local to the web server rather than add more data to the core systems. The core systems were overloaded anyway, and moving functionality away from them enabled a faster service to the customer.

In addition, log files and audit files were easier to write to a local store rather than trying to fit them in to the core systems. Thus was born the concept of a front end that customers interacted with, and back end databases that stored data local to that individual channel.

Operational Data Store (ODS)

Next is the operational data store. An operational data store typically sits just downstream of the operational system and its back end database. The premise is this:

- The fulfillment system has a back-end database, but this is used for fulfillment – it is constantly in use meeting customer needs.

- However we have a requirement for short term reporting. An example may be "how a call centre queue varies over the day" or "the number of complaints currently in-progress and how many of these have been resolved within the day." Other examples may be "how many customer enquiries turned into firm orders in the last hour", etc.

- This "intraday" reporting is not necessarily served by a data warehouse (of which more later), as the data transfer to a data warehouse is typically done end of day. So we can't use this. For really good survival-of-the-business reasons you don't want to run reporting off the fulfillment systems. Those critical systems need to be dedicated to the task of keeping the business running.

- So there is a requirement for a database that receives a feed on a very regular basis (either immediate or very short time) that can be used for intraday reporting.

This is an ODS. Note an ODS typically holds very little data – it can either delete data after a period (typically 24-48 hours) or alternatively can pass data on to the data warehouse at end of day and then delete.

Data Warehouse

So, if that's a back end database and an ODS, what is a data warehouse? Put very simply, a data warehouse is a large database. But what is specific about a data warehouse?

Typically data warehouses are used for:

- Historical data. Storing many years of data is very expensive computationally. Therefore a normal database, that might be the back end to an application, will slow down as the number of records gets larger and larger. Therefore it is common to offload the data (for example once a day or month) into a database that is more optimised for large amounts of historical data.

■ Aggregation from back end systems. A typical organisation may contain many hundreds of databases, each with their own data structure. If an organisation wants a "360 degree view" then it may wish to join the data from many product systems. This requires a place where all the data can be stored, ideally in a identical format.

The data warehouse sits between the operational systems and provides a platform for analytics and reporting.

But, basically it's a large database.

DataMart

A datamart is a database that normally sits downstream of a data warehouse and normally contains a subset of the total warehouse data. Typically it might be the data that is related to one division, or just one country.

Why do datamarts exist? Its another result of the "not everything is best at everything" problem.

A fundamental problem with data is that the structure necessary for write performance is not the same as the structure necessary for read performance. To write to a database as efficiently as possible, the best scenario is that every piece of data is only written once and writes are made in parallel. This typically means data is split up into many tables in a warehouse, a processes known as normalisation.

However, reporting and analytics requires data to be joined together. It is generally not possible to run reporting and analytics directly off the back of a warehouse, because:

■ Table joins are expensive in terms of compute time. For example, if you can imagine obtaining data for one customer from ten tables. Armed with a customer number you need to search through each of ten tables. Even worse, imagine trying to get the details for customer orders?

- Go to table 1, get the orders,
- then take that data to table 2, and search down for the order details,
- then go to table 3 and search for item descriptions,
- then go to table 4 and search for prices.
- then combine it all
- It would take forever.

- So datamarts are designed so all the data is dumped from the warehouse into the mart, but its transformed en route so that it makes subsequent joining and querying easier.

- It also reduces the number of users interacting directly with the warehouse. Ideally the number of users interacting directly with the warehouse should be nil. Why? Because the warehouse is optimised for write, and it should be left to do that job.

- It also saves time. The amount of data in a warehouse makes it computationally expensive to run queries. Searching through 50 years of invoices takes ages. However if you know there's a datamart with just the invoices from the last year, that's a lot faster.

So a datamart reduces load on the warehouse, and also results in a better and more individualised service to the consumers of data.

Data Consumption

Finally, we need to cover data consumption, where data is actually used. Data consumption is where the end users start to see the data. Typically these divide into reports on one hand, and direct use – in some way – of the data on the other. I will cover these all in more detail later.

Reports are static documents that are provided to the end user. There are a number of ways in which reports can be generated out of the data store.

Direct Querying

Direct querying represents a scenario where an application allows a user to run queries directly against the datamart and return results.

Pre-configured Reports

Pre-configured reports are pre-built reports that are generated by a script or stored procedure. They run against the database – often at times outside the normal office hours – and are then saved into a common area for access by others in the organisation when they are ready to do so.

A BI (Business Intelligence) Layer

A Business Intelligence layer is a data store automatically provisioned with data, but within the data store users have a more or less free rein to create reports and discover data.

Visualisation Tools

Humans process visual data far better than lists of values. Using visualisation tooling enables data analysts to create associations between data far quicker than would be possible otherwise.

AI and ML

A very topical element of data consumption is artificial intelligence and machine learning. I will go into this in more detail in a later chapter, but for now it can be regarded as "another data consumer." It mostly uses a lot of data to draw conclusions that would not necessarily be easily identified otherwise. It tends to be computationally expensive.

End User Computing

End user computing is one of the larger uncontrolled and unmanaged areas within most organisations. The growth has been partially fueled by the inability of end users to gain the information they need out of the main systems, either due to lack of access to the data, lack of flexibility, or poor data quality. The increasing power of desktop and laptop computers and tablets – hand in hand with the ease of use, intuitive interfaces and accessibility of desktop productivity tools, has meant that each individual is often their own report writer, business intelligence guru and data architect.

This, of course, has advantages for the individual, but now many reporting structures in most organisations are based on data and application constructs which are undocumented, uncontrolled, have massive critical person vulnerabilities, and are equally extremely likely to have large errors. It is common for reporting to be based on "George's Spreadsheet" or "Ann's Database" which – if the organisation is lucky – will be held on a shared (and hence backed up) drive but more likely resides on the local hard drive of a PC or laptop, ready to be forever destroyed by an errant cup of coffee.

This is typical in environments where data architecture is poor, as business users, unable to obtain data directly out of source systems, will extract the best fitting data they can, and then play with it until it meets requirements. This is one of the reasons why having poor data architecture increases organisational risk.

Summary

The above chapter has covered a high level tour of the common components of data architecture. With the exception of the channel component, each area will be covered in much more depth later in the book.

At this point the reader should have a high level sketch of the components that they may expect to find as a practicing data architect.

What we will do now is to do a deep dive into the components that are the specialism of the data architect.

Chapter 11: Deep Dive: Databases

What's a Database?

OK, so lets stat at the beginning. The basic building block of data architecture is a database. But what's a database?

A database at its most basic is an application that acts as a store for data. It is an application that runs on an operating system that runs on a physical machine. So, in short, its an app.

What does this app do? Well, it allows a user to store data in some form of structure. That structure is customisable by the user (to an extent) and the app allows access to that data. So it's a bit like an app that creates the (virtual) shelves in a library.

Most database applications also include other functionality - a database manager. This allows the database administrator (DBA - a human role) to create new databases, manage databases, and perform tasks such as creating, storing, updating and deleting data. So the app allows extensions to the database library, and also contains automatic processes so when you tell the app to store information at a particular location, the app can do it.

Talking of the particular location, the app also creates indexes, so information can be found again without having to search the entire library.

The database manager also (generally) will interpret instructions that are written in an appropriate language and translate these into actions on the actual data. The most widely used language is SQL (Structured Query language, normally pronounced "Sequal").

What is important to note here is that the way in which the database is structured and the way in which these instructions are written can massively change the performance of your database. A user will not wait half a day to add a new customer to the customer table. They won't wait half a day to get a current balance. Therefore the structure of the database is critical.

There are several types of databases. Why? Because there is a fundamental problem with databases, and that's that there is not such thing as a single database structure that does everything well.

As I have said before, it's a bit like cars. A car that is designed to go off-road will have certain tyres (knobbly) and generally lots of clearance and lots of suspension travel. A car that is designed to go 250mph will have smooth tyres and hug the ground. Fundamental physics means that it is not possible to have a car that does both as well as a car that is optimised for either one or the other.

It's the same with databases. You cannot have a database that is optimised for high volume writes and also have the same database optimised for high volume read. Equally, flexibility comes at a performance price. The more adaptable and changeable a database is, then the slower queries will take. Or, possibly more accurately, the harder it is to make the database performant.

As a result there are a lot of database products on the market that do various things well. There is no one-size-fits-all.

What I will do in this chapter is to go through the various types of database and explain the advantages and disadvantages. Broadly, I will cover traditional relational databases and the (many) various types of non-relational (often called NoSQL) databases, plus a few outliers.

However, a couple of important acronyms require explaining before I get into the detail. Unfortunately this can come across as quite technical, so please forgive me. However it is essential to know if you are making decisions between different types of databases.

ACID

ACID is a characteristic of some databases. It de-acronomyns to Atomic, Consistent, Isolated and Durable. But what does that actually mean?

- Atomic means a transaction (such as updating a customer address) either completes or doesn't. There is no middle state for an ACID database. This principle needs to apply regardless of crashes, errors or power outages.

- Consistent means any change meets data integrity requirements or it gets rolled back. The data integrity requirements will vary from one database to another, but an example is a constraint that every customer must have a surname. So if a name change occurs that does not include a surname, not only will it not be written to the database, but *no part* of that change will be written to the database and it will be highlighted to an operator as an error.

- Isolation means what you do to one bit of data doesn't affect other bits of data. So changing my name does not affect your name.

- Durability means once its done, it stays done. It doesn't subsequently change unless an action is taken to change it.

For most data requirements ACID is absolutely essential. Corrupted data can take a long time to be noticed, and the damage to an organisation – and the cost to fix – can be astronomical. ACID databases ensure that data keeps integrity.

In fact, ACID requirements are so fundamental to database design that they are often not thought about at all.

BASE

BASE stands for Basically Available, Soft State, Eventually Consistent

- Basically Available. That the data is there and able to be accessed, even in the event of failure.

- Soft State. That changes may occur over time even with no input.

- Eventually Consistent. This means that the database will not necessarily be consistent after every transaction, but will eventually become consistent over time if no further changes are made.

Why does BASE exist? BASE exists because some non-relational databases don't support ACID and a way of describing their operation was needed. Note the important differences between ACID and BASE.

CAP Theorem

The CAP theorem relates to distributed databases – where – for performance reasons, resiliency, or any other reason, various parts of the database need to reside in different locations. Each part of the database may be called a "shard" or "node."

In this case CAP de-acronymises to:

- Consistency: Consistency means that all users see the same data regardless of which node or shard they connect to. For this to happen, data that is written to one node or shard must be immediately written to all the others before the transaction is deemed 'successful.' Otherwise the write must be rolled back (similar to "C" in ACID.)

- Availability: Availability means a user request for data will get a response, even if one or more nodes have failed.

- Partition tolerance: This means that the database will continue to work even if there is a breakdown in communication between the various nodes.

The CAP theory states that in any distributed database no more than two out of the above three can be achieved at any time.

I have covered the above here as the above three acronyms are key to understanding databases, and it is worth spending a bit of time to go into them in more depth. However I would strongly suggest that a Data Architect do their own research covering ACID, BASE and CAP as they are not the focus of this book which is intended as a general introduction.

Standard Relational Databases

Standard relational databases are what everyone thinks of when they think of databases. These are the databases that have been around for decades. In fact, for a long time they were synonymous with the word "database." Data is ordered into "tables" which have columns (called attributes or fields) and rows (or records). Each table is connected to other tables via "keys" which are reference fields that ensure each entry is unique.

Example

Customer Table

Customer No (Primary Key)	Name	Date of Birth	Address
C0001	John Smith	1/1/1970	1 Station Road
C0002	Peter Jones	2/4/1975	42 High Street

Product Table

Product No (Primary Key)	Description	Price
P0001	20kg Bag of Sand	£5
P0002	Shelf Bracket	£1

Orders Table

Order Number (Primary Key)	Customer No (Foreign Key)	Product No (Foreign Key)	Quantity
A0001	C0001	P0001	10
A0002	C0002	P0002	2

All of this is very standard and exactly what people think of when they think of a "table" in a database. Looking at the above, and using the "keys" to map between the tables, you can see that John Smith bought 10 Bags of Sand and Peter Jones bought 2 shelf brackets. So far, so simple, and that's – with few modifications – exactly how databases have operated for over 50 years.

Further tables might include detailed descriptions of the products, or the quantity that is held in the warehouse.

A relational database has a number of advantages and disadvantages.

Advantages
- Well understood. Relational databases have been used for decades. The base table structure (rows and columns) is ubiquitous through many applications.
- Consistency. Relational databases are very good at keeping data ACID. They normally contain a lot of checks and balances to ensure that this is the case. For example, a relational database management system will commonly "lock" a row so that if one process is working on making a change, no other change can happen to that record until the first process has finished. This prevents two processes trying to simultaneously update the same data.
- Standard Query Language. SQL ("Structured Query Language") is widely – almost universally – used across relational databases.
- Long history means general reliability and stability are excellent.

Disadvantages
- Creating and maintaining the structure takes time and effort. In a relational database the structure - many tables linked together by primary and foreign keys - needs to be created and managed. Designing the structure can often take considerable time but results in a better output for the user (see data modelling).
- Because of the above - the structure - there are constraints on what can be stored in any one database. You (generally) cannot put a picture in the same column as text.
- Scalability can be difficult. Relational databases tend to a complexity limit where performance starts to suffer. In addition, the typical way to scale them is to add more hardware which is expensive.

- Generally not distributable. Few if any relational databases are able to shard like NoSQL databases (of which more later).
- Adding data structures is more complex and introduces redundancy. For example, if you wish to add an attribute to a single row, then you need to add a column, therefore, for that column, one row is populated and all other rows are null (note "null" means "not populated").
- From an evolution point of view, relational databases don't move much. There are few new capabilities being added.

Therefore it was to provide an answer to some of the drawbacks of relational databases that non-relational databases were developed.

NoSQL Databases

> **Note:**
>
> "NoSQL" can be used to say "not SQL" or "Not Only SQL" depending on the vendor.

Although they were originally developed in the 1990s non-relational (commonly called "NoSQL") databases really gained wider acceptance in the early 2000s. There are many types on the market, and whilst they operate in different ways, they don't have the constraints of relational databases.

The appeal of NoSQL databases is flexibility and cost. Many are open source so "free" to download and run. Also, their ease of implementation is a draw. Many are very easy to create and run. So, in theory, a free download of a fully functional database from the vendor, and a few clicks on a mouse, and the database is up and running.

"NoSQL" however is a collective term. There are many types of NoSQL database, and here I'll cover the advantages and disadvantages of each.

> **Note:**
>
> As a result of the very low bar to access, unfortunately they are often used when a relational database would better fit the use case. I will pick up on this later.

Key Value Databases

One of the earliest (and simplist) forms of NoSQL database was the Key-Value database. Data is held in key-value pairs in what is essentially a very long list in one "table." The key is unique, the value can be anything.

Key	Value
Customer_1	John Smith
Customer_2	Peter Jones
Customer_3	Anne Parker

In many key-value databases the "value" can vary significantly. It can contain more information than one line of text, for example below;

Customer_1	Name: John Smith DOB 1/1/1970 Address: 1 Station Road

Alternatively, the "value" may be a picture, video, or any other type of digital construct.

The database doesn't really know or care very much about the contents of the "value." The database manager software is given a "key," and returns a "value." As a result simple database operations are very fast.

Another big advantage is that these databases are extensible. Increasing the information within a "value" for a single record is trivial. This compares with adding an attribute in a relational database which may involve changing the structure and adding another "column" – essentially adding the value for every record.

Advantages

- Flexible data model. Adding another value to a "row" is as simple as updating the value. The schema is totally flexible and can grow with the organisation.
- Performance can be exceptional, though with the caution it depends what you are trying to do. If you are trying to run a relational work-

load then it may be much slower than a relational database. However non-relational workloads are often very fast.

- Open source. Many NoSQL databases are open source, and as a result require minimal initial investment. Whether Total Cost Of Ownership (TCO) is comparable with proprietary databases is not examined or opined on here. However the initial outlay is lower so the barrier to entry is lower.

- One big advantage of key-value databases is that they are very easy to horizontally scale. A degree of explanation is required here. Sharding is a way of adding another database *beside* the one you already have, on different hardware, and potentially in a different location. However the two databases look like one database to any user, and operate as one database. Each "part" of the database is called a "shard." This allows rapid and effective upscaling of performance. You can double the hardware supporting the database very easily. Not only that, there is often no limit to the number of "shards." Sharding is generally used to support very large datasets and/or high query volumes.

- NoSQL databases are evolving fast, so that capabilities that did not exist a year ago may already have been added by many vendors. In fact this is indeed the case, even over the period of writing this book there has been a huge jump forward in the capabilities of NoSQL databases. Relational database capabilities have, in comparison, remained relatively static.

Disadvantages
- Limited functionality. As the database manager doesn't really know what is inside each value, what can be done is limited to returning a value from a key. You generally cannot query within the value – inputting the key, returns the value, you can't search inside the value.

- Not suited to relational workloads. "Relational" workloads involve joining data using keys. In a NoSQL database this can be computationally extremely expensive, if possible at all.

- Often does not support ACID. In fact, BASE was coined for NoSQL Databases. So if atomicity, consistency, durability and Isolation are necessary, a NoSQL database is not necessarily for you. It also means you have to accept the limitations of BASE, and have to consider whether BASE meets your use case.

- Standardisation. There are lots of NoSQL databases and mostly they all work in different ways. There are also lots of relational databases, but mostly they all operate identically. The comparative newness of NoSQL means fast evolution and fast change, and the industry hasn't yet settled to a clear set of standards.

- ■ Security. Whereas security comes as standard in relational databases, it is not necessarily the same for NoSQL databases. This is partly a product of the speed of evolution, but also a product of the prioritisation towards performance and scalability.

Document Stores

Document stores are very similar to key-value databases. The difference is the "value" is actually structured or semi-structured data - referred to as a "document." An example could be a JSON (Java) document. Each document is indexed via a unique ID. The big difference is when data is accessed, the data can be accessed directly from inside the document. So unlike a key-value database, you can look "inside" the actual value, and the structure is richer. A document store could be considered a half-way house between a relational store and a key-value store.

Key	Document
Customer0001	\<customer name: John Smith\> \<Date of Birth : 01/01/1970\> \<Address: 1 Station Road\>
Customer0002	\<customer name: Peter Jones\> \<Date of Birth : 02/04/1975\> \<Address: 42 High Street\>

The document is extensible in the same way as a key-value database. The schema is variable, and adding a value for one record does not mean you have to add a record for every one.

Key	Document
Customer0001	\<customer name: John Smith\> \<Date of Birth : 01/01/1970\> \<Address: 1 Station Road\>

Key	Document
Customer0002	<customer name: Peter Jones> <Date of Birth : 02/04/1975> <Address: 42 High Street> <Hair Colour: Brown>

Advantages

- Flexible record structure across the database. There is no need to keep the same structure for every record as is the case in a relational database.
- Much more powerful than key-value databases as you can search and retrieve information from inside the document.
- Performance and scalability - can be very fast to populate, given all you need is a unique ID and the document itself. You don't need to know much about the data internal structure. Many relational databases have constraints which force data into particular formats so that it is consistent, this is not necessary in a document database (to an extent, and depending on the use).
- Open Source (as is the case for most NoSQL Databases)
- Rapidly evolving (as is the case for most NoSQL databases). New functionality is being developed all the time.

Disadvantages

- Again, the database is not suited to relational workloads. If you need to interlink the documents – essentially if your use case is relational – then the database is going to get very complex very quickly. So an example where you have to pick all orders from a certain year and then determine the contents of the order, how much it costs, and who it was dispatched to, would take multiple reads and a long time. Saying that, it would be possible to build a document store that easily and efficiently met this use case, but then you would have a similar problem if you wanted to know which customers lived in which town. In short, if you need a relational workload, use a relational database.
- As per key-value databases often does not support ACID.
- As per key-value databases standardisation issues.
- As per key-value databases security issues.

Graph Databases

The next type of NoSQL database I will cover is the graph database. Graph databases store data as nodes and relationships. This is a very different storage approach to any other database. These databases specialise in workloads where there is a very high level of connectivity between each record, and the connectivity, in itself, has meaning. A typical example is a social network.

An example of a node might be an individual, and an example of a relationship might be "parent" or "work colleague." These datasets are characterised by their highly interconnected nature – in fact, in a way the connections are the most important part.

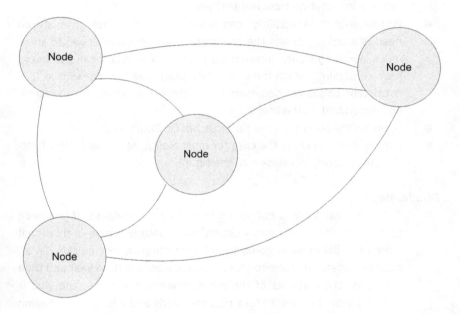

These databases excel at use cases where traditional databases – and most NoSQL databases - fail badly. To find out who connects to who at five levels of separation would require highly complex and massively computationally expensive workloads in traditional or NoSQL databases. Graph databases can perform this kind of analysis easily.

Advantages
- Can be very fast for graph related use cases – areas where typical relational and NoSQL databases struggle. In fact, if you have this kind of

use case at any scale beyond the very small then a graph database is often the only answer.

- Some graph databases support ACID transactions.

Disadvantages

- Rapidly evolving. Graph databases are new, and the landscape is not very mature. A good side is new capabilities are continuously coming on the market, but the bad side is stability. The next release may work totally differently to the current release. These databases are at the revolutionary rather than evolutionary stage. This can result in a continuously steep learning curve.
- Difficult to scale. Graph databases are currently more difficult to scale than other NoSQL databases – however, as to the point above, this is changing rapidly.
- No common query language. Each graph databases may use a totally different language to query the data.
- Security and encryption are currently (again, see comment about rapid evolution) not supported or poorly supported.

In short, graph databases are very good at the specific use case where data is characterised by nodes and relationships. However, for other use cases they are likely to be inappropriate.

Columnar Databases

The last main type of NoSQL database is the column store database. At a high level, the main difference is that data is arranged into columns rather than rows. So the database is optimised for retrieval of columns.

Advantages

- Performance. Often in query operations you don't want to use the *whole row* for **one** record, but the *whole column* for **all the records**. Columnar databases – because of the way they store the data – facilitate this. Some queries as a result – those that relate to a single column – for example totalling invoice values – can be very fast. Columar databases allow you to avoid touching irrelevant data.
- Scalability. Similar to other noSQL databases columnar databases are easy to horizontally scale.
- Compression. Columnar databases benefit for greater compression abil-

ities and hence can speed up read operations. They are very good for analytics.

- Flexibility – adding an additional column is as easy as adding an additional row in row-based databases.

Disadvantages

- Doesn't support relational workloads. Or, more accurately, doesn't support row-based workloads. So, for getting all the columns for one entity, each column would potentially have to be read individually. In essence it is the inverse problem to that of relational databases, where retrieving a row is very fast. In short, the more fields you need to read, the worse the performance gets.
- Writes can be very onerous as for each "record" multiple writes have to occur as each column is "written" separately.

In-Memory

As a sidenote It is worth mentioning "in-memory" databases. These are not a separate database type as such - any relational or non-relational database can be in-memory - but a function of the hardware on which the databases run.

Databases can be slow because there are a lot of read and write operations to disk – commonly traditional spinning disk drives. Whilst the advent of solid state drives have vastly sped up these kinds of operations, an "in-memory" database takes this a step further and moves the whole database, the management systems and all the data, into RAM (Random Access Memory).

The decrease in price of RAM over time has meant that this is possible. This allows databases to exist that are incredibly fast. Typically, without the time penalty of having to access disks, microsecond access times are possible.

The disadvantage is they are potentially ephemeral – data in RAM only exists when it is powered, so turning off the server would result in a total loss of data. They are also – per unit of storage – much more expensive than traditional databases.

However, if your use case requires extremely high speed, they may be the best choice.

Making the Database Choice

I mentioned above that there is no one-size-fits-all when it comes to databases. Therefore the type of database, and its internal structure, needs to be optimised for its use. The data architect needs to make choices, balancing the pros and cons of each type of database, and then further choices based on the internal structure required. In almost all instances, compromises will be required.

Relational Databases

It may sound a little obvious, but if you have a relational workload, then choose a relational database. If you are joining a lot of data together then this is the database for you. Relational databases tend to be good for write, and – depending on the data model – less good for read, unless they are optimized that way. So having one warehouse for read and one for write, with transforms in the middle, is the way it has been traditionally done for decades. Also, if your transactions need to be ACID, then this is the database for you.

Key-value Databases

Good for basic and simple data storage, even if the number of items is huge. One of the most scalable databases, and very easy to write to, but would not cope with a complex query load.

Document Databases

Probably the best compromise, giving some of the advantages of relational databases but also some of the advantages of key-value stores in terms of flexibility and scalability. Comes with the health warning that transactions may not be ACID.

Graph Databases

Graph databases are great for graph workloads. These are workloads where there are many nodes and relationships, and there are "many to many" connections – a type of relationship that traditional databases don't cope well with at all. The best way of looking at this would be "if your data looks or feels like a social network, then a graph database is probably a good solution."

Columnar Databases

Choose Columnar databases for analytic workloads where you are only looking at a small number of attributes at one time. Avoid if the workload involves a lot of "row-type" writes, unless you are happy for the performance payoff for fast analytics being slow update.

Important Note

A warning. All databases require compromise. This is fundamental to the nature of data. This has not stopped many companies in the marketplace promising revolutionary databases that will solve for every compromise with no downside. Mostly, these companies are selling snake oil.

Decide on your use case. Identify the database that meets the use case. Test it. Make sure it works before committing.

Summary

In this chapter I have performed a deep dive into databases. Databases are the "bread and butter" of the data architect, and a degree of expertise will be expected by any employer.

Many data architects are specialists, with deep knowledge of one type of database, others are generalists. New types of databases – and new interpretations of the old – are coming on the market all the time, so keeping up with recent developments is essential for the data architect in practice.

Whilst saying the above, this chapter is merely scratching the surface. I have books on my bookshelf that dedicate *three thousand pages* to *one* version of *one* database. Databases are really complex. There is a lot to know. Most data architects thankfully do not need this detail. However having in-depth knowledge of one type of commonly used database is advantageous.

Chapter 12: Deep Dive: Data in Motion

Introduction

If databases are one side of the basic bread and butter for the data architect, the other is data in motion. As is the case for databases, there are many ways this can be done, and each method has different advantages and disadvantages.

In this chapter I will cover the most common ways that data can be moved around an organisation. I will cover:

- Traditional ETL (Extract Transform Load)
- APIs (Application Programming Interfaces)
- CDC (Change Data Capture)
- Replication
- Streaming

I will also cover the tricky subject of timing, which applies to all of the above.

Traditional ETL

ETL stands for "extract – transform – load" and pretty much does what it says on the tin. It extracts data out of a source system, transforms it (if required) and then loads it into a target system.

ETL may be "push" – where the source database runs a process which dumps a selection of records out to a file, or "pull" where the ETL application hooks into the source and extracts what is required. Regardless, a selection of records is copied, placed in a file, and moved from the database itself to a target (which may be another database), which reads the file and then performs a process on the records, which may be simply to store them again.

It is common for a specialist application to manage both the process on extraction and load, and the transformation in the middle, rather than it being run by either end. There are many of these types of application on the market. They fundamentally contain a set of instructions describing what is needed from the source and where it is located, what is needed in the target and where to put it, and what to do in the middle, plus code that will perform the transfer.

The typical pattern is there will normally be a fixed source (with a fixed IP address, a database structure, and source fields) and a fixed target (with a fixed location, a database structure and target fields. This is shown in the example below.

Source Database

Type: SQL Server
Location: 10.0.0.1

Target Database

Type: SQL Server
Location: 10.0.0.2

Source Table	Field	Transform	Target Table	Field
CustomerDetails	Forename		Cusdetail	Firstname
CustomerDetails	Surname		Cusdetail	FamilyName
CustomerDetails	DOB	MM/DD/YY to DD/MM/YYYY	Cusdetail	DateOfBirth
CustomerDetails	Postcode		Cusdetail	P_Code

ETL is by far the simplest way in which data can be moved from A to B.

Discussion on Timing

Batch

Much of the way that data systems work comes from the early days of computing. Computer systems (historically) were in use serving customers from 9am to 5pm, and then after this period – after the working day was over – the systems would perform maintenance, patching and upgrades. It was also a time for running the big jobs that would adversely impact fufillment if run during working hours. These kind of jobs include transfer of data between systems.

The advantage of waiting until the end of the day to perform these ETL transfers was a clean break to the data and no further change would occur until the next working day.

Big data transfers were (and are to this day) compute-intensive. If run during the working day, there was a chance that load on the systems would cause the normal business work to slow down or, worse, stop, with customers unable to interact with the company.

However in all markets the working day is extending. Companies with physical premises often open earlier than 9am and close much later than 5pm. Large shops will open untill 8pm as a norm, Call centres typically open untill 8pm or 10pm. Many supermarkets run 24 hours, and of course any business that allows ordering over the internet may accept 24-hr ordering.

This is quite apart from any business that operates in more than one time zone, which has to deal with continuous operation.

This move to "always-on" has been a huge challenge for IT systems. The traditional maintenance window has shrunk, and more and more operations have to be performed during the working day, and this may include data transfers. Adaption has been required.

Traditional ETL was the old end-of-day solution. A common problem as the window shrunk was the "batch not finishing" – resulting in an incomplete or corrupted file. Typically phraseology was "batch failing." When this occurred, the batch had to be re-run. Of course the problems then got bigger the next day, as there was now twice as much data to transfer. It was perfectly possible to get into a rolling failure scenario where the downstream system never caught up, resulting in hard decisions for database managers.

Microbatch

One way to get around this problem of the "big batch job" is to use microbatch. This is exactly the same as the "end of day" batch, but rather than one big batch run at the end of the day, lots of batches are run throughout the day. To give a sense of scale, "microbatch" generally refers to transfers down to about

5 minute timescales, which is good enough for almost any business reporting use.

The big advantage of microbatch is cheapness of implementation and effectiveness of impact. Cost may be as low as simply changing the time interval on an existing scheduled job. The impact is the business can now look at intraday reporting, and will probably consider the data "real time" (see separate section on real time").

The disadvantage is that you are adding work to the fufillment systems during the working day. The idea of microbatch is the load is small enough to not create a noticeable effect or overload, but care needs to be taken.

> **Andecdote**
>
> It is perfectly possible – indeed I have seen it in practice – where due to the fufillment systens nearing capacity a microbatch running every 15 minutes never completed. The system then tried to start the next batch with the previous batch still running, hence slowing it down further. This had a knock on effect with the result the system crashed and outage occurred across the organisation.

APIs (Application Programming Interfaces)

The API revolution started around 20 years ago and continues to this day. Application Programming Interfaces are slightly confusing and deserve their own explanation.

At its most simple, an API is a set of re-useable instructions that allow computers to move data around. The data that is moved around is based on a conversation between computers. An example would be:

Computer 1: "Hi, what service do you offer?"
Computer 2: "If you come to me with a customer number, I will give you the address for that customer."
Computer 1: "Great, can I have the address for Customer Number 123456?"
Computer 2: "Sure, its 1 Station Road, London, W1 4QG"

There's normally some formatting instructions included as well.

Computer 2: "If you come to me with a customer number in this format, I will give you the address for that customer in this format."

The API sits in between the source data repository and **any** consumer. So any consumer that is authorised to use the API can submit a request and get the data it needs.

How does this affect data transmission?

- Because any authorised party can come to the API endpoint and request data, the "point to point" element of data transmission is removed.
- There is no scheduling – the request can happen at any time.
- The format is fixed.
- The source system only gets one type of request for the data.
- The source system has a single interface that "talks its language"

API Architectures

Given this can be a little confusing, its worth a little more explanation. In short, the consumer connects to a gateway, that will deal with initial handing of the query. It will operate according to instructions for API use (called "contracts") , as well as dealing with traffic management.

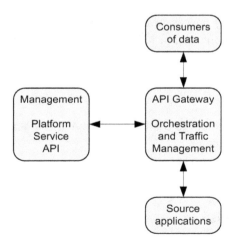

The result is a re-useable means of obtaining data from a system that is clear to use, always provides data in the same format, minimises load, and removes the need for every consuming system to write its own requests.

System and Process APIs

Having dealt with the basic overview, lets delve into a bit more detail. You may have heard of system APIs and process APIs (SAPI/PAPI).

A system API interacts with back end systems. Back end systems are often different from each other. In fact, generally each one is "special" with its own data model, its own column names and table names, its own formats and obviously its own location.

A system API is an API that is crafted for that particular system. However, it presents its results to the outside world in a "standard" format. The advantage is that the system itself can be changed, and the consumers of that system would know nothing and not have to change any of their interfaces. It isolates downstream consumers from needing to worry about the internal processes and data structures of the source.

However, what if a business process needed data from more than one system? Here you need a process API.

An example might be if a business process (for example a website that presented "order history" to the customer) needed to connect to both the customer system (for the order numbers) and then a fufillment system (for the details of each order)

So a process API would then call two system APIs:

- It would supply the customer number to the CRM system API, and get back a list of orders for that customer
- It would then send this list of order numbers to the fufillment system, which would return the orders.

So what about Experience APIs?

The third type of API is the experience API. This is one level up again. An experience API solves for the problem "but what if a whole load of data consumers all want basically the same data, but they all want it slightly differently?"

Experience APIs will connect to process APIs to deliver data to the consumer in the way that the consumer needs it.

A full "orchestration chain" would therefore be: Back end system > System API > Process API > Experience API > Consuming system.

CDC

The next method for moving data around is CDC. CDC stands for Change Data Capture. This is a process that supports real time transmission of change. The process – which is often performed by the source database itself – identifies when a change has been made to data and records the change. The change may then be used to update another database (to keep, for example, a backup database in sync with a primary) or to send downstream.

There are a number of ways of performing CDC but I won't go into detail here. At a high level, however, we have:

- Using the database log file and scanning this.
- Row/column scanning for changes
- Timestamps
- Row versioning

CDC commonly uses an agent (small program) which is run by the database management engine and monitors the database for changes. It then identifies that change and propagates it to a downstream system.

The big advantage is timing. CDC is instant or near instant. The disadvantage is having the agent running increases the load on the database.

Replication

Replication is similar to CDC but often done on a more granular level. The goal of replication is to ensure that two databases are identical. This is generally used for backup purposes in a hot/hot or hot/warm environment where instant failover to a second database needs to be in place.

The replication is often done within the database system itself, and the database management program is configured so that every change is written twice. Replication is expensive computationally, and of course requires similar underlying hardware on both systems.

However, because of industry demands for backup and safe failover, replication is extremely common, and most database vendors will supply products to perform replication.

Streaming

We have to date talked about data that moves from a static location to another static location, via a pipe that may be a traditional ETL, or an API. What if data doesn't work that way?

Let us take an example. Say an organisation wants to know if a customer changes address, and furthermore wants to know if they move to a "sanctioned country." This is something that needs to be flagged immediately.

One way this could be done is by taking a copy of the customer address file every day and comparing it to the previous days' file. Those addresses that did not match would be changes. These changes could then be extracted and analysed to see what the new country was.

This approach is entirely possible, but very, very hard work. It also introduces a delay in the process, and is a huge load on the system. Typically this kind of extract would be done out of hours, but with an increasing move to 24 hour working a "downtime" window may not exist.

Alternatively the source system could "emit" a small packet of data every time there is an address change. This packet of data could contain information on the change and its nature, together with old and new addresses. It could publish this data packet, and anyone who wanted to know about address changes – anyone in the company – could subscribe to that "stream" of events.

This is how streaming systems work. Systems publish "events" into "topics" (e.g. "address changes") to which consumers can "subscribe." It is entirely up to the consumer what they do with the events. They could save every one down into a database, they can inspect each event and drop those which do not interest them, and save the rest, or even take those events that they are interested in and themselves stream them elsewhere. All the source system is responsible for is creating the stream.

The advantages of streaming services are many. As explained above, it is possible to save a lot of heavy lifting in obtaining extracts. Its also faster – streaming services are typically real time or near-real-time. So reaction to the events can be faster too. This is really important in time-sensitive use cases such as fraud. Finally, it is good news for the source system, as the source system only has to emit once and after that all the problems are at the consumers end.

Disadvantages of Streaming

Ordering and integrity are key here. In a normal ETL, there is a conversation between the source and the target. The conversation goes on the lines of:

Computer 1: "I've sent 45,012 records, how many have you received?"
Computer 2: "I've received 45,012 records, that's cool, you can consider this transaction complete"

With streaming there isn't that integrity check – if an "event" goes missing in transit – through a momentary network outage, system error or similar – not only is there no way necessarily to tell, but there's also no mechanism within the stream for an individual consumer to ask for a resend.

A second problem is around ordering. In many streaming systems, there's no way to tell if one message should come ahead or behind another. This may not be important in certain circumstances – for example the address change example above. However if the stream is of transactions, and the receiving system is looking to amalgamate these into a running balance, then errors can occur. Some streaming systems do have mechanisms to get around this – numbering the events means that ordering can be determined and missing events identified – but not all systems do this.

Real Time vs Non-real Time

It is worth making a side point here about "real time" as it often causes confusion. Business units and IT both use the words but rarely do they mean the same thing.

Real time, from an IT point of view, means instant. Certainly under a second, preferably substantially lower than that down to microsecond timescales. In large IT systems the amount of investment required to support this kind of response is very large. In large multinational corporations this may be very difficult due to the processing time at each end of a data transfer and simply the time data takes to move around the world.

Near-real-time is slower – typically in the range of a few seconds up to a few minutes. Near real time is generally achievable at a reasonable cost.

One of the mistakes often made by businesses is to call for "real time" performance without there really being any business need for it. Something I have seen a lot is a call for "real time" reporting. Realistically is the business likely to be able to react so fast that reporting has to be up to date to below a second? No. Within a few minutes is more than enough.

Therefore demanding "real time" reporting is doing very little but raising the cost of implementation. The cost rises exponentially as the required timescale gets shorter. Actual "real time" reporting may cost 10x the amount of near-real-time with absolutely no business benefit. Therefore be wary of any requirements that state "real-time."

Summary

Moving data around an organisation is an essential part of its operation. There are many ways of doing this, and each has advantages and disadvantages. In this chapter I have covered most of the ways in which data can be moved, and delved in some detail into exactly how they work.

In general, the simpler and slower the means of moving data used, the cheaper and easier it is to implement. Moving to real-time data propagation (such as CDC or streaming) significantly raises costs as opposed to ETL/batch processes.

The choice of what to use will be based on the business requirements and is definitely the domain of the data architect.

Chapter 13: Deep Dive: Reporting and Visualisation

Introduction

Having covered the different types of database, and how databases connect to each other and how data can be moved around the organisation, I'm now going to go into more detail on reporting and visualisation .

As I said in an earlier chapter, there are many ways in which data can be consumed.

- Direct Queries
- Canned Reports
- A BI Layer
- Visualisation
- Analytics
- AI/ML

Each has their own advantages and disadvantages so each has their place depending on the use case. In this chapter I will cover these in a little more detail. However it should be noted that this is a huge area. Entire books have been written on this area, and indeed on subsections of this area. I would strongly recommend the budding data architect reads widely.

This area is very important. If we consider the end users to be the "customers" of the data architect, the quality of the final deliverable - both in terms of data and the way it is delivered - is critical to the consumer's view of the data architect and the data delivery chain as a whole. A business user is not likely to care if one type of database is used rather than another (providing performance is not impacted), as they cannot see that functionality. However they will absolutely have a view if the reporting solution does not deliver the data they need, in the format they need, to perform their day to day role. Spending time in this area to ensure the end users are pleased with the data deliverable is key to success for a data architect.

I will cover the different forms of reporting and visualisation in turn.

Direct Queries

Direct querying represents a scenario where an application allows a business user to run queries directly against a database and return results. The business user would have an application on their machine – or may remotely log in to another machine – which has the access privileges to submit queries to the database administration engine which will then run the queries against the database.

The advantage is that this is extremely powerful, and allows the user total control over the information they require.

The disadvantage is that you need a tech-savvy user to understand the complexity within a raw database. The user needs to have a detailed knowledge of the table and field names within the database, how they inter-relate, and be aware of the primary and foreign keys (assuming a relational database here, but similar data for NoSQL databases). The user must thoroughly understand the data model and the data contained within the database.

Not only is this very detailed information, it is very specific information that is likely to be true for that database and that database only. It is information that is difficult to acquire, and only an individual who has spent long time working with the data and the database will be able to get good results.

There are also massive risks with this approach:

- The main one is that a user with direct access to the data can cause carnage. They can obliterate years of history, they can change data any way they see fit. It is, in many cases, at best a very bad idea, at worst an existential risk to the organisation. An accidental deletion of the entire customer database may take years to fix and is a self-imposed disaster.

- Even giving a user read-only access to the data isn't much better, as they can run queries that slow down the database, or even cause it to crash.

As a result, direct querying of a database is almost never seen. The number of individuals with the ability to directly interact with the database is limited to the very minimum, via very tightly controlled and privileged accounts.

I only mentioned it here to explain that it should be never used and (almost) never is. It only takes one mistyped letter in a SQL query and the database may fall over. As a result, access to a database is almost always restricted to system-level scripts which run without the possibility human error – or human malignancy - being involved.

Canned Reports

Pre-configured reports are a way around this problem. The business gives the IT team requirements and the IT team builds the reports which are automated and run by scripts or stored procedures. The reports are tested to make sure they don't crash the database and are automatically output to a shared area which business users can access.

The reports may be available at a certain time every day or may be run ad-hoc when the business users wish to do so. The average business professional hates this way of creating reports as it gives them no flexibility. The average IT professional loves it, for pretty much the same reason.

There is however absolutely a place for this kind of report. Many reports do not change month-to-month and contain standard information in a standard format. Examples may be:

- The sales report for the week/month
- Available cash
- Profitability
- Current stock reports
- Bank account balances
- Service level reports.

.. and many more.

In fact, these kind of reports are common in most organisations. It is only when the regular report highlights an anomaly that further investigation is needed.

Saying that, there are dangers here too.

- There is a tendency for consumers to think that the reports are "correct" if they show minimal variance from the previous month. It is very easy for this thinking to continue even when there is a known major reason for variance. So, if a fire disrupts production, but an error in the reporting means it reports the same figures as last month, a mental leap is needed to look at the figures and ask "is this how they should look given what we know about the business?" Assuming the computer figures are correct is a bias that has resulted in a lot of incorrect conclusions.

- The second danger is that the reports continue to be produced long after anyone reads them. Because they are produced automatically and faithfully dropped on the shared drive every week/month, and are created by an automatic script that runs without any manual intervention, it is often the case that many reports are not actively used any more. Often a high proportion – I've seen 90% - of canned reports are never used, but they continue to run and continue to consume valuable IT resources.

- Lastly, canned reports need to be updated. So if the business changes then the script needs to be updated. An example I have seen is where a new product was not added to the script, so was missed when the sales report was run. Because of the characteristics of the organization, this resulted in a multi-million USD cost.

However, saying all of the above, canned reporting is the mainstay of most organisations.

Business Intelligence (BI) Layer

A Business Intelligence Layer is a half way house, where the business users are given meaningful links into a reporting engine which allows arms-length access to the data. The IT department will transfer data to a data store with information that the business users require. The data transferred to the store will be based on requirements that business consumers supply to IT. The required data will then be transferred on a regular basis – daily, hourly, real-time, whatever is required.

The business users are then given free rein to create queries with this data but only have access to the provisioned data store, not the underlying source.

There are a number of valuable advantages.

- Meaningful data.

    I mentioned "meaningful links." One common problem with many databases is that the names of data fields are often not overly helpful when it comes to actual business meaning. Typically this is because the number of characters for field names is strictly limited, so there is no scope for a business-consumable descriptive text. Most field names are abbreviations, and by necessity abbreviations cannot give all information.

    If you are lucky you may see "CUST_BAL" as a field name in a database which is - probably - customer balance. But when is that balance? Now? Last night? Last month? Does it include accrued interest? We don't know.

    Equally, "CUST_ADRS" is probably customer address, but residential, postal? Its probably residential but we don't know.

    There are remarkably few totally unambiguous fields ("CUST_DOB" being one). Without a full understanding of the meaning it is very easy to end up using the wrong data and making incorrect decisions.

    What a business intelligence layer does is create a repository of data with defined meaning. First of all, the fieldnames should be "translated" from the source database into something more helpful (e.g. Customer_Current_Residential_Address) and due diligence should be performed so that the field it is coming from actually represents that truth.

- Isolation

    The second advantage is isolation. Whilst the data comes from the warehouse, it is now in an isolated silo. This is a reasonable compromise that enables the business users to play with the information but allows the IT staff a reasonable assurance that they will not be pulled off their lunch because someone has run a query that has taken the source database down.

Saying all of this, there are also several disadvantages

- Timeliness

A common problem with this kind of construct is timeliness. There may be an end of day transfer from the source system to the warehouse, and another end of day transfer from the warehouse to the BI layer. As a result all the data is two days out of date. This may be frustrating for the business whose monthly reporting is very tightly controlled in terms of time.

I will give an example: Typically senior execs will want to make decisions as fast as possible, so if they are only hearing about issues after a week (2 days IT processing, 2 days analysis, 1 day to put the shiny exec presentation together) then they may be unhappy. In reality reporting by working day 5 is – in many organisations – a unachievable nirvana, and typically – with data processing, double checking and collation from various parts of the organisation - reporting by working day 20 is more likely to represent practical reality.

This lag between the business events occurring and the business management knowing about them is a key problem for organisations. An event that occurs on 1st January would form part of the January report to executives that may not be delivered until 20th February - six weeks after the event and far too late for the management to do anything about it.

A key role of the data architect is to understand the business needs in terms of timeliness and design a data architecture that supports them.

- Can turn into a swamp

Because the business can design their own reports, and potentially write the results back into the same location, and these reports can then be used by others, it is entirely possible for the pool of data to turn into an ungoverened swap. This rapidly builds to a level of undocumented complexity so no-one knows what data it contains, what data is accurate, and what is not. The common name for this is a "data swamp" and brings to mind images of data users struggling through dirty data to try and find what they need.

As with EUCs, it is easy for the business to end up relying on "Dan's report" or "Sue's Data Extract" which creates a key person dependency and, depending on the degree to which transformations are allowed, possibly no-one – apart from the author – knowing what the report actually shows.

Therefore, if a BI layer is used, data governance is key.

BI Layer Tools

If we accept that a Business Intelligence Layer is one of the best solutions for both business and IT, in terms of balancing value to the business and risk to the organisation, it is worth a brief discussion of the tools that sit above that layer. These tools divide into:

- Canned reporting
  It is of course perfectly possible to run canned reporting from a BI layer as easily as from a data warehouse. The operation is identical – and has the same advantages and disadvantages – as running canned reports direct from a warehouse.

- Visualisation tooling
  A very popular way of analyzing and presenting data is visualisation tooling. The way these tools typically work is they take a snapshot of the data and then let the user play around with it as they see fit, holding the data in local computer memory to allow fast reporting and manipulation. Typical players at present are:

  - Qlik
  - Tableau
  - Cognos
  - Google (with Data Studio)
  - AWS (with QuickSight)

These visualisation tools are very powerful. They are designed to take large data sets and make them understandable, and also allow users to quickly build dashboards that are both slick, seamless, and very well presented. Typical functionality includes automatic creation of graphs, pie charts, area graphs, timelines, and complex graphical representations that will highlight a particular facet of the data.

Most will also allow a drill down into the actual detail rows of the data set, so that an individual anomaly can be identified and investigated. In many cases this is as simple as double-clicking on an individual value in a graph.

Visualisation tools are highly effective and deservedly have wide adoption. Their disadvantage is mostly that they need to keep the data locally and they do not query underlying databases directly.

- There is therefore a need for significant processing power on the local machine. This can cause scaling issues when dealing with large data sets.
- Data is "refreshed" - essentially updated from the underlying database to the local machine - on a regular basis - so often the timeliness is no better than ETL.
- Some of the tools are better than others at joining data sets. Therefore complicated logic may have to be performed on the underlying dataset before it is transferred to the visualisation engine.

However, their wide adoption is a testament to their effectiveness.

Analytics

I have divided analytics into a separate section as by "analytics" I refer to advanced understanding and querying of the data in order to derive insights that will help the organisation. The description "Data Science" is often used for this kind of analytics. For the purposes of this book this is seen as very separate from both canned reporting, and visualisation, though the latter can certainly stray into the "analytics" space.

Analytics as a capability will typically be characterized by looking at large data sets - potentially many billions of rows, potentially trillions of data points, and looking for patterns between them in order to offer insight and improve the performance of the organisation.

As such, analytics users almost always require data at a high level of granularity - and will typically want to access the "raw" data. Many organisations create a separate data storage area for analytics, and provision that area with powerful tooling that is capable of processing very large data sets.

Analytics tooling is one of the growth areas in data. There are many tools on the market. The variation is often between ease of use and power. So those tools where the user has to write code to manipulate data sets are the most powerful, but offer a high learning curve, whereas more user-friendly tooling is less powerful.

At the time of writing key open source tools are "R" - a statistical analysis language and "python", which is a general purpose programming language which has become popular for data analytics. Most cloud providers will enable the provision of these alongside their own tooling.

AI and ML

One area that needs explaining but is somewhat different from others is AI (Artificial Intelligence) and ML (Machine Learning).

AI and ML are very much, at the time of writing, more used as buzzwords for complicated algorithms rather than having the meaning that might be inferred by a non-technical person, that of artifical brains and self-learning machines understanding and processing data. There are a few - very few - true implementations of either at the time of writing.

Machine Learning

So, what do I mean here? First of all, let us take machine learning. The way this generally works is that a problem is identified that it is difficult to solve. A good example is identifying what is in a picture. It is difficult to do this via a computer simply scanning an image as pictures can be very different. So a machine learning process is used. The process is as follows:

- A "training set" is created with a large number of pictures.
- Human beings then will classify pictures into categories.

- A computer reads in all the pictures and also the classifications given by human operators.
- The computer is fed a new set of pictures, and, based on the training set, makes a guess at classifying the pictures.
- This guess is then corrected again by humans.
- The process repeats until the computer reaches a desired accuracy.

Is it true "machine learning" as would be described by any sci-fi novel? Not really. It is however a very useful way of solving otherwise difficult problems which would otherwise require human intervention.

Artificial Intelligence

In a similar way artificial intelligence is also often misnamed. AI is often little more than a large number of pre-programmed algorithms which give the user the impression that they are interacting with an "intelligence." AI is typically used as a term for chatbots, where really all the AI application is doing is recognising a wide range of text input, and then using algorithms to select the correct output. Again, useful, but not "Artificial intelligence" in the sense of science fiction.

It is, of course, possible to combine both machine learning and artificial intelligence, so that an AI programme takes the responses it receives from interacrions with users and pattern matches to obtain what it believes is the "right" result, and then repeats the process. Unfettered this kind of system is very "leadable" and several organisations have discovered that malicious individuals can "trick" the AI into using inappropriate language.

"True AI" when it comes, will be a revolution, but we are not there as yet.

Summary

In this chapter I have given an overview of the different ways that data can be consumed.

Again, due to space limitations, I have not covered this topic is high detail. I would strongly recommend that if interested in this area the reader looks for one of the many publications which go into much greater depth, as not only this chapter merely scratching the surface, but this is an area which is changing all the time, as it is at the forefront of development.

For the data architect, this area is a constant trade-off between business desires, ease of implementation, and risk to the organisation, and is often where the most heated arguments occur.

However, as stated earlier, it is also critical to the data architect and the business, as it is the area where consumers of the data finally see the results of the entire data pipeline.

Chapter 14: Deep Dive: Cloud

Introduction

So, we have talked about "what is a database?" We have talked about how a database works and common types. We have talked about data flow, and the basic building blocks of data architecture. There's one area we have not touched on yet and that's the physical hardware which underpins all data constructs.

This is especially relevant in relation to public cloud infrastructure, which has introduced entirely novel architectural concepts and new ways of working over the last few years.

In order to be a good data architect, detailed knowledge of these areas is not required. However basic knowledge is essential, as public cloud has wide adoption precisely because of its revolutionary impact and for this reason I am including this section in the book.

I would go even further, and state that for a data architect working in the mid-2020s it is strongly advisable for career progression to gain as a minimum the entry-level qualifications from the major cloud providers.

History Recap

I will start this chapter with a brief history recap. In the 1980s organisations housed computers in specialist buildings within their own premises. The buildings had to be specialist as computers like environments that are cool and clean. These were the first "data centres."

These data centres were initially managed by the organisation that used them – which meant a steep learning curve and often relatively inefficient implementations, as the organisations were not specialists in the area.

The general pattern was that an application (such as a database) would be hosted on a dedicated physical server running a dedicated operating system.

This arrangement is called a "dedicated host" – as the underlying hardware and operating system are dedicated to hosting the application – in this case a database. However it is very inefficient. One database may be running at 100% capacity whilst another may be running at 5%. The solution to this problem was virtualisation – which started as long ago as the 1960s but really only exploded as a technology in the 1990s. In a virtualised environment hardware resources are shared amongst more than one operating system.

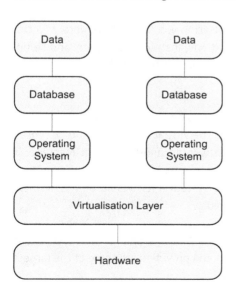

Here we have a "virtualised host" - the advantage here is resources can be shared, and utilised more efficiently. The virtualisation layer "fools" each operating system into thinking they have their own dedicated hardware, and shares resources between each. In fact each database can be allocated a specific amount of RAM, CPU, and hard drive space from the pool of actual physical resources on the physical host machine.

Virtualisation is extremely common. In fact, it is so common that it is the default for data centres globally. Having a "dedicated host" – i.e. physical hardware that is dedicated to an individual application - is getting increasingly rare, and is largely only relevant now to specialist use cases.

Back to the history, even in a virtualised environment, the organisation would still run its own hardware. This specialist activity could be far away from the organisation's key competency, and require many specialist staff and high investment in IT infrastructure. It was still not an ideal solution.

The next stage in evolution was for certain organisations to specialize in running data centres, and other companies would rent space. They would still have their own IT hardware, but it would be installed in someone else's building, and the third party would be paid to keep the building secure, cool, and provide backup power in the event of loss.

The specialist IT staff within the organisation would log in remotely to the server and perform administrative operations, install applications, and so on. Whilst the staff would still be required, much of the overhead in running a dedicated data centre was removed.

The next stage was for the hardware itself to be rented. The data centre provider would create a virtual machine and the virtual machine would be rented by the organisation. If the organisation wanted another virtual machine, it could be created in seconds. The organisation had total control of what was done on the machine, but the operating system itself would be maintained, patched and run by the data centre provider.

Thus came the beginnings of public cloud. Cloud is one of the most recent seismic shifts in IT. At the time of writing, the providers are some of the largest organisations globally:

- Google (Google Cloud Platform)
- Amazon (Amazon Web Services)
- Microsoft (Azure)

This has created a significant shift in the way that organisations work. Firstly, organisations can concentrate on what they are good at, rather than running data centers, and running data centres can be left to people who specialise in this area.

Secondly, the companies that are providing these services are often large – and have operations in many countries and many locations within each country. As a result resilience is increased. It is much easier to have a back-up site if the only work needed is for the provider to duplicate something it is already running on commodity hardware and software to another site. Equally expansion to another continent is as simple as a few mouse clicks to duplicate the running hardware and software in another area.

Thirdly, barriers to entry are reduced. A start-up company no longer has to create a data centre – it can simply rent one. This has been proved time and again as small start-ups have achieved global scale rapidly.

Tiers of Operation

The public cloud providers normally has three tiers of operation.

Infrastructure as a Service (Iaas).

In this model a virtual machine is supplied and the organisation manages everything on that machine. The virtual machine runs on physical machines that are housed in the cloud provider's data centres. The cloud provider will spin up a virtual machine within minutes of the request from the consuming organisation. The consuming organisation can then log into the machine and has full control including the responsibility of managing the operating system.

Platform as a Service (Paas)

In this model the platform (operating system or similar) is also provided, and the renting organisation only supplies and runs the application (and its associated data). An example might be that the organisation is given a location where it can log into and install and run its database. The responsibility for running the operating system is with the provider. The responsibility for running – and patching and maintaining – the database is with the client.

Software as a Service (SaaS)

Lastly, you have software as a service, where everything is provided by the third party. The customer only provides its data.

Example

The cloud provider supplies login information and a location for a database. The database is operated and patched and maintained by the cloud provider, and the consuming organisation ("client") simply uses it to store data. The client has no need to worry whether the underlying operating system is patched to the latest security standards, nor does it have to care about the hardware resources. All of that work is performed by the cloud provider.

The client does need to care about cost though. The cost to the client of the service will include built in costs for hardware and platform, so although it is not separately managed by the client, it does have to be paid for.

How Does it Work?

Setting Up

Note

By far the best way to learn about public cloud are the many free courses and hands-on tutorials run by the cloud providers. This is unfortunately a subject that is difficult to cover in text. Therefore I would strongly advise a reader, wishing to learn of the area, to spend some time working through some basic tutorials.

The typical approach to set up services in cloud is to use a "console" created by the cloud service provider. This is a user friendly graphical user interface on a web page – and within that web page the user can choose between a large number of services.

At its most basic, the user will choose to create a virtual machine, with certain parameters – RAM, CPU, etc. On pressing a button within the webpage marked "deploy" instructions will be sent to a data centre and a virtual machine will be set up, all without the intervention of any human agency.

This can happen very fast. Typically within 60 seconds the machine is up and running and ready for the user to log in remotely and start working. Of course, the clock also starts ticking on the costs, which are incurred by the second and billed monthly.

Use of the Webpage/GUI/console is very user-friendly. However, anything you do on a computer can be automated, so it is possible to automate the creation of virtual machines on cloud. You can also automate the creation of networks, the creation of software, and similar. All it requires is a script (text file) that can be processed by the cloud provider.

It is now perfectly possible to have a set of instructions in a script that will create a data centre of thousands of computers, set up to an organisation's precise specifications, in minutes. If the data centre goes down – for any reason – then the script can be run and another, identical data centre can be created a few minutes later – ready to use and with all connections in place.

This concept is called "infrastructure as code."

Cloud Concepts

As cloud has evolved and the services have become more mature, cloud has spawned its own terminology and capabilities. I will cover a few of these here.

■ Serverless

I have explained most of the above in terms of a virtual machine, but the cloud landscape has evolved far past this point. As mentioned previously Software-as-a-Service operates where the only thing the client has to provide is data. But this can go further – where the server is totally transparent, and what is provided is simply a "thing that runs code." This is called "serverless."

I am not going to give much more detail here as it is a mode of operation more applied to running code than specific data applications. The user logs in to a specific location, runs the code, and then exits. But these small functions are used to move data around so its worth knowing that this is possible.

- Auto-scaling.

This is a process where the capacity of a system is automatically increased as the workload increases. Normally, as workload increases on a server performance starts to degrade as it nears capacity. However with auto-scaling additional servers can be automatically created to share the workload.

Obviously there is a cost to this. In addition, some architectural components such as load balancers need to be created, but it allows a seamless increase in capacity that will allow for high period of usage. Equally, when the usage drops, the servers can be automatically turned off and the organisation stops paying for them.

- Containerisation

Lastly it is worth covering a few words on containerisation. Containerisation is a little like an extreme form of virtualisation. It isn't specific to cloud, but is commonly used in cloud environments as containers can be quickly created and put into production.

A container is a subset of an operating system, that contains all the elements needed to run an application and *nothing else*. Containers can be moved between machines, and provide an answer to the problem of "well it runs fine on my machine."

Containers also allow rapid replication and hence scaling of applications. If your application is getting overwhelmed by demand then a second application running in a container can be created much quicker than duplicating the entire virtual machine.

They also provide a secure environment for developers to create applications, and also a way to share those applications – and everything that is needed to run them.

Advantages of Cloud Computing.

Cloud computing has become widespread as it offers many advantages - and very few disadvantages - compared with traditional organisation-run data centres. In this section I will cover the key advantages.

- Concentration on core capabilities.
  The organisation using the service is not providing hardware. Mostly, companies are not experts in buying and running hardware. Their expertise lies elsewhere, in whatever they produce or do. Letting the cloud providers operate in their expertise areas means the organisation can concentrate on its own area of expertise.

- Networking Flexibility
  It is often said that cloud computing can function as an extension of the organisation's internal network. In fact, the number of potential networking configurations that can exist is pretty much infinite. A network on the cloud can be configured to have private spaces, semi-private spaces and public spaces. Traffic can be routed wherever the customer wishes.

- Resiliency
  The resiliency of cloud systems is typically many times what can be achieved on a typical on-premises system. There are various reasons for this, but chiefly:

  - The cloud providers – Google, Amazon, Microsoft – grew out of a world where massive scale was required, and downtime would not be tolerated. The systems they created were designed to hardly ever go down, and if they did, to be back up quickly.
  - Typically in a traditional data centre, "high" resiliency would be "five nines" (99.999% uptime) or "six nines" (99.9999%). The latter equates to 31.5 seconds of downtime a year. A few years ago this would be considered exceptional resiliency.
  - Cloud providers operate at a different level. Google advertises "eleven nines" – 99.9999999% uptime. This equates to roughly one second downtime every 3,000 years. In fact resiliency is one of the key positives of moving to cloud.

- Multi-region and global

  Another area where cloud excels is when an organisation wants to operate across a wide geographical area. The flexibility cloud provides is a game changer. In a previous traditional environment, to set up an operation on a different continent an organisation would either have to accept that customers on that continent would have degraded performance in terms of access time, or would have to enter into an agreement with a data centre in the remote location to host a duplicate of their systems.

  Cloud providers make this incredibly easy. To set up a server in the USA from the UK, or vice versa, or almost any country in the world, takes exactly the same time as setting up a server in the same country – normally around 60-90 seconds from pressing "deploy" to be being able to log in and start work. I have personal experience of this.

  Building entire stacks of systems, networking them all together and making them available takes the same time as if it was in the same country. In short, an organisation can become global with as much effort as setting up systems in their own garage. In fact, probably less.

- Software constantly evolving

  The number of actual "products" that can be supplied by most cloud providers is vast, ever changing, and covers a huge range of capabilities.

  Products are continually being released and evolving. Whether it be machine learning, databases, artificial intelligence, or simply something as mundane as a different way of configuring a virtual machine. It means that any company that is cloud based has at its fingertips a range of software from the bleeding edge and newly developed, to the tried and tested and stable. The organisation is free to experiment as much or as little as it wishes.

Disadvantages

The main disadvantage of cloud computing is cost. Though cloud is likely to be a lot less expensive in general than an organisation running its own data centre, any organisation using cloud needs to understand that costs can increase rapidly.

For example, if autoscaling is switched on and a user runs a very complex query involving a huge dataset, and the back end auto-scales to ensure the query works, running that query can cost tens of thousands of dollars/pounds/ euros. In fact in one organisation I'm aware of exactly this happened and a single query cost $30,000. So configuration must be carefully controlled. If the same happened on-premises the server would simply have crashed, which could have been its own set of issues, but would at least have kept the hardware cost down.

Other disadvantages include:

- Control – you are not in control of your environment to the same degree that you would be running a server on your own premises.

- Ownership – you'll never "own" the hardware. There will never be a point where you will fully own the hardware and the monthly cost will stop. In that sense its akin to leasing a car as opposed to buying a car. Obviously, to continue the car analogy, in a traditional loan repayment you may well find that when the car is eventually yours after many years of repayments then its in such poor repair that you need another. In which case there's no advantage in "owning" it at all.

- Extremely large data transfers can be clunky. The speed of data transfer is limited to the connectivity available, and in relation to very large data sets even the fastest of modern interconnects can be slow. Most cloud providers offer a way around this - typically a truck turning up with a very large storage device onboard and plugging directly into the organisation's systems, transferring the data, and then driving back to the cloud provider's data centre and plugging in here. However, it should be noted this is only really necessary for *extremely* large transfers.

Summary

Cloud computing has been a game changer to the IT industry. The cloud revolution has been incredibly beneficial to many organisations, from the large to the small.

It means that small start-ups have access to exactly the same hardware resources as large multinationals, and the barrier to entry to many markets has been reduced. For large corporations there is the opportunity for increased efficiency and concentration on what they are good at, rather than spending valuable resources running data centres.

As stated above, it is strongly recommended that any data architect invests time leaning about public cloud offerings and also obtaining "cloud architect" certifications.

Chapter 15: Deep Dive: Data Ecosystems

Introduction

Having gone through all the various types of data component in a little more detail – and accepting that it is perfectly possible to write one – or many – books on each, it is worth mentioning a couple of outlying data constructs on the market. One is very common, the other is less common and relatively new.

The first is a Data Lake, the second is a Data Fabric.

Because these types of data construct draw together many different parts of the data journey into a whole, I have decided to cover these under "data ecosystems."

Data Lakes

The data lake addresses some of the issues with both traditional ETL and traditional warehouses.

Part of the problem with a traditional data warehouse is that a lot of effort required to transform data on ingest. The source system data has to be mapped to the data model that is used in the warehouse. This work is typically very onerous. However much of this work is often wasted as not all of the data that is transferred to the warehouse is used. In addition, the data warehouse will refuse data that is not in a proscribed format, so voice and video files, or unstructured data, often do not fit easily into the data warehouse.

The solution to this was the "data lake", where the philosophy was extract, load and transform, rather than extract, transform and load. So raw copies of the data would be loaded into the data lake, and then, if they were needed for downstream use, would be mapped or transformed *on exit*, rather than *on entrance*. The intention was to save time and be more efficient and quicker to delivery.

Physically, a data lake is a large storage facility – often based on open source architecture (Hadoop is the most popular product at time of writing) – where all the data in the organisation is stored, in the same format as the source systems. In addition to internal data, the data lake may contain additional data from social media, reference organisations such as the government or proprietary websites, or the Internet in general. Key concepts are:

- Any data can be thrown in and the data store is not going to break as a result.
- A data lake enables an organisation to add data to their overall store easily and quickly, with all the worrying about how it will be used to come at a later date.
- The data lake enables greater analytic flexibility as the analysts are not constrained to just the conformed data in the data warehouse.
- A data lake decouples the generally unstructured and ad hoc process of discovery and mining from the formal and rigid processes of regulatory and financial reporting.

There are, however, disadvantages of a data lake architecture:

- Tracing lineage of data is often difficult or impossible.
- Governing data is often difficult or impossible.
- Working out the right data to use is often difficult or impossible.
- All eggs are in one basket. If a hacker gains access to the data lake then they have access to everything in the lake.
- Control of access is critical.
- Metadata management is key.

A Gartner article, recent at the time of writing this book, noted wryly that:

"there are no barriers to entry into many data lakes."

A subsequent blog post added:

"By its definition, a data lake accepts any data, without oversight or governance. Without descriptive metadata and a mechanism to maintain it, the data lake risks turning into a data swamp"

Technology

It is, of course, possible to have a "data lake" under any technology. If you consider the basic principle of a data lake is "ELT" rather than "ETL" then any ELT approach will work. However data lakes have historically been based on the Hadoop ecosystem. This can run either on premises or the cloud.

Because of the many common implementations of Hadoop and its ecosystem, for completeness the various elements of the Hadoop ecosystem are described below. This gives the reader an idea of the different components of a data lake and how they work.

- HDFS. Hadoop Distributed File System. HDFS is the part of the system that allows for the distribution of data across many nodes. This is key to the operation of Hadoop, and the orchestration of the many nodes into one connected ecosystem.
- HCatalog; Hcatalog is a metadata layer that allows the user to understand what data is held within the Hadoop ecosystem.
- MapReduce: MapReduce is the way in which Hadoop processes large data sets. It is a two stage process: Stage 1, "Map", takes the data and splits it up into manageable chunks. Stage 2, "Reduce", takes each chunk and applies processing to that chunk. All the reduce jobs are being run in parallel, so that vast data sets can be processed, or queried, in a reasonable timeframe.
- Yarn: "Yet Another Resource Negotiator": Yarn manages resources across the ecosystem.
- Hive: Hive is a data warehouse system that is used for large datasets. It takes commands in its own language (HQL) and translates these into MapReduce jobs that can be run against the mass dataset.
- Pig: This is a platform for processing and analyzing large data sets.
- Spark: Spark is a data analytics platform. The platform is designed to be able to process and analyse very large data sets quickly.
- Zookeeper: This allows co-ordination of distributed applications.
- Squoop: Squoop is a tool for transferring data from one database into the Hadoop ecosystem. It is, at its most basic, an extract-and-load tool.
- Flume: Flume is used for aggregating and collating log data.
- HBase: This component is a NoSQL distributed database designed to store structured data at large scale.

it should be noted, however, that new components are being added all the time. In addition, the above components are designed to work as a unit, a seamless data ecosystem that meets business needs.

Data Fabric

A relatively new data ecosystem is the data fabric. A data fabric looks to provide a consistent architecture across a number of systems through to a number of consumption points. The idea is that no matter where the source system is located, whether it be on premises, or on multiple cloud providers, all the data is integrated into an ecosystem. The users don't need to worry about gaining access to source systems, or even in translating the meaning of the different values, it is all done for them.

A data fabric bundles in a number of specific capabilities that cover functions of the data ecosystem, including ETL, warehousing, a business intelligence layer, a data dictionary, a data catalogue, etc.

Data Movement, Discovery and Storage Components

- Data discovery.
  Where is your data on your network? Many organizations simply don't know where their data is stored, The data fabric can search the network to identify databases and then catalogue them. Direct connections can then be established – subject to security clearances – to get access to the data and bring it into the data fabric.
- Ingestion:
  Some form of accelerated ingestion of data from common sources. Typically this involves connectors to many of the most common database types that allow the fabric to connect to the database, display its contents, and then enables a user to pull data in to the fabric for consumption.
- Auto-mapping.
  When bringing in data from a source system, a data fabric may automatically map the data to common business terms, such as "customer name" or "credit card number." This work is commonly done by pattern matching - for example 16 digit numbers are commonly card numbers – and keyword matching on the field name. This auto-mapping can be highly effective, especially if a degree of machine learning is per-

formed, and it can reduce manual effort considerably. Accuracy rates of 80%+ are possible.

Data Consumption Components

- Data catalogue.
  A catalogue of all the data accessible within the data fabric – essentially a description of all the data that exists at a granular level. This may extend to a "data marketplace" where the data can be chosen, and accessed, and reported and analyzed.
- Semantic layer:
  A semantic layer provides a consistency of meaning from a number of underlying disparate source systems. This ensures, for example, that customer balance form one system has the same meaning as a customer a balance from another system.
- Distribution:
  A means of enabling a user to connect to the data and move it to a place of their choosing – whether it be a local hard drive or datamart, or analysis platform. This distribution method needs to be easy, intuitive and ideally very much based around a graphical user interface so that no code is required.
- Visualisation:
  Data fabrics generally will incorporate some form of visualisation software in order to display data. They may borrow from existing software, or have one of their own.

Data Management Components

- Data entitlement management.
  Who is able to access what data for what? User data access is often managed on the fly, so that if a data user submits a query for data they are not entitled to access, the query will give a nill return – or a partial return based on what data they are able to access.
- Anonymisation.
  Masking data so that even if lost there is limited data risk. Most users in an organisation have no reason to know granular detailed information such as customer name or customer address. Equally, actual card numbers are only needed by a few. Anonymisation/masking protects data from all users but those who need to know.

- Data Quality:
  Measurement of data quality in systems – commonly known as data profiling. This covers the type of data in each field, the frequency of the various data types, anomalies, default values and so on.
- Tenancy.
  Allowing multiple areas of the organisation to have logically separate parts of the data fabric so that they can work as if in their own silo, whilst also having the benefit of a wider distributed system. This is especially relevant in global systems where data residency laws may mean that some country data has to be on premises, and for others it resides on cloud.
- Lineage:
  Being able to track the way that data flows through the organisation is increasingly important in order for decision makers to be able to be sure that the data they are making decisions on is correct. It is also an increasing focus of many regulators, to ensure that organisations can control and understand their data. Data lineage functionality enables a user to trace the data they are using back to its original source.

Technology

It is possible to build a data fabric in almost any technology, as realistically a data fabric is an orchestration of existing capabilities rather then new technology of itself. Saying this, cloud scale technologies do lend themselves very well to data fabric implementations.

The advantage of the data fabric is that it is a "one stop shop" for solving the problem of "lots of data all over the place" and bringing it together.

Architecture

Although there are many variants, at a high level, data is ingested into the data fabric via a mostly traditional ingestion processes. Most data fabric providers include a large number of connection options to all the major database vendors. The difference here is that when the data is ingested it will normally be automatically mapped to a consistent data model, and also added to the catalogue and marketplace.

The same applies in relation to lineage and quality. Often lineage – where the data comes from and how it traverses through the fabric - will be recorded automatically, as well as profiling the data to determine its quality and conformance with consistent formatting.

> **Note:**
>
> Quality profiling can never tell you whether data is accurate – as in "is an accurate representation of the real world" – but can tell you whether the data is consistent.

Advantages

The big advantage is that all the data capabilities are organised into one coherent whole. Rather than the organisation having to take a number of suppliers and orchestrate a solution with a lot of complex interfaces, all this is done for you in advance by the data fabric supplier.

As such implementation can be faster to get to a given point and that point often offers a greater degree of interaction and integration for an organisation than if they had done the work themselves.

Disadvantages

There are a few key disadvantages to the data fabric concept, but as noted this is an area that is continuously changing. At the time of writing, key disadvantages include:

- Scalability can be a problem. It depends on the complexity of the data fabric, but very high CPU and memory load can result if the fabric is trying to do too much with data, especially in relation to ingest, where profiling, lineage and visualisation can all be quite resource intensive.
- Cost. Data Fabrics can be very expensive.
- Tie in to a vendor. If a fabric is not modular, or has interdependencies between its capabilities, then it can be difficult to use different vendors for different parts of the fabric. No organisation is the best at every part of the data ecosystem, and if it is not possible to swap in and swap out components the organisation can be stuck with sub-optimal components in some areas of the implementation.

Summary

The data industry is continually evolving, and new products come onto the market all the time. Many of these look to solve fundamental issues around ease of use, efficiency, evolving business or regulatory requirements.

Data lakes have been established over the last 5-10 years, data fabrics are more recent. Both look to bring together a number of capabilities that were traditionally separate, allowing for easier and faster implementation.

However both are not without pitfalls, and the data architect needs to make a considered decision on whether they will meet the organisations needs. It is very easy for the desire for "new and shiny" to outweigh the needs of practicality. So whilst - in their place - they are both good choices, the place needs to be the right one.

Chapter 16: Deep Dive: Management of Third Parties

Introduction

Up to this point in the book, we have covered, almost exclusively, data that is created within the organisation in question. This data is clearly within the remit of the data architect, and the data architect will need to curate and manage the data flow to ensure that business needs are met.

However it is perfectly possible for an organisation to outsource data functions. In this case, the overall data architecture is not fully managed by the organisation concerned. This brings with it risks. This chapter looks to explain these risks and how to mitigate them.

More and more organisations are moving from Corporate Information Manufacture to Corporate Information Assembly. In Corporate Information Assembly, information is manufactured elsewhere by third parties and delivered to organisations and locked together to create value and insight. This brings a new set of challenges for the organisation - both operationally - as organisations that use information are no longer present at the start of its lifecycle, but it also challenges data architecture, data management and data governance.

So how should organisations govern this new paradigm?

Here I look back 25 years to when - in a previous life - I was an auditor and performing a stocktake at a machine assembly plant. The company ordered parts from third parties which it then assembled. When parts arrived from suppliers they were x-rayed to detect internal cracks, carefully measured and checked if they met specification, before being passed for use.

The Corporate Information Assembly Plant needs to do the same, as information imported into the organisation brings with it risks: These can include, but are no way limited to:

- Supply of incorrect data, resulting in poor decision making, time spent on data cleansing or poor customer experience.
- Supply of correct data but in a wrong format, resulting in time spent to rectify.
- Supply of data with a different meaning to that which the organisation expects (as a result of poor understanding of requirements) resulting in incomplete understanding of the data and poor decision making.
- Supply of correct data too late.
- Legal or regulatory breach or loss of reputation due to any of the above.

Whilst it does depend on the relative negotiating power between the supplier and the receiving organisation, the receiving organisation should, if possible, write data principles and management requirements into contracts and take steps to ensure compliance. But what approach can we use to ensure a comprehensive coverage? If we consider the familiar DAMA framework, we can use this as an effective checklist.

- Architecture Management
- Data Development
- Database Operations Management
- Data Security Management
- Reference and Master Data Management
- Data Warehousing and BI Management
- Metadata Management
- Data Quality Management

Data Supplier Responsibilities

Architecture Management

Any substantial organisation should have an architecture management function. Unfortunately many organisations, when considering third party data, simply plug third party data into the architecture with no consideration of architectural principles or governance. The third party needs to demonstrate how it will:

- Align with the organisation enterprise data model and business models.
- Define technology architectures, infrastructure architectures, metadata architectures and data architectures.

- Supply information at the same level of granularity as is expected by the recipient.

Data Development

- The data model that is used by the third party is outside the control of the receiving organisation, however meaning is critical to effective interfacing. In the absence of the Utopian ideal of a universal data model, meaning differs for data fields across organisations. For example:
  - A field that is named "current balance" may or may not include accrued interest or charges.
  - A claim amount may or may not include a deduction for excess.

The supplying organisation should semantically align with the recipient's expectations. Otherwise it sets up confusion across the receiving organisation where information is no longer consistent and trust in the information landscape is undermined.

Database Operations Management

The third party needs to demonstrate that it will manage its databases in accordance with good practice. It is not acceptable that a third party can simply state that the contractual deliverable is supplied data in a specific format. The propensity of the supplier to deliver bad data partly depends on the quality of the management of databases within its control. This will include, but is not limited to:

- Control of database environments
- Backup and recovery
- Database performance levels
- Database service delivery
- Non-functional requirements
- Data lifecycle management including retention, archiving and purge of data
- Adequate control over technology licensing

Data Security Management

It should be a necessity of business to business interaction that the third party adheres to data security requirements of the recipient organisation. The supplied data may be either confidential and/or sensitive. Loss, theft, or inappropriate access will pose as great a risk as if the loss were from the recipient organisation systems themselves. The third party needs to meet the recipient organisation's criteria in terms of, but not limited to:

- Data security controls and procedures
- Secure storage
- Encryption standards
- Management of users and passwords
- Management of authentication and access behaviour

Reference and Master Data Management

Whilst less critical in terms of reputational damage, it is still important that the third party is aligned with the recipient organisation in respect of reference data and master data. This will include compliance with country lists, product lists, and allowable entries in terms of title, postcode, and similar.

It should not be up to the receiving organisation to translate a seven level address into a five field one.

Data Warehousing and BI Management

If we make the assumption that the data model and reference data alignment have already taken place then in theory, data from a supplier should seamlessly merge with that of the recipient organisation. At the point where such data is loaded into a data warehouse or is mined by a business intelligence function then the data should be fit for purpose.

Metadata Management

The third party needs to demonstrate how it will match the metadata standards of the recipient organisation. The third party will need to supply to the recipient organisation information on:
- The type and kind of metadata that will be supplied
- Data dictionaries where the data does not exactly meet the recipients definition, data model, hierarchies or reference data

- Formats
- Traceability information such as creator, date/time, source
- Lineage where appropriate

Data Quality Management

The supplier needs to ensure that the data supplied is of an appropriate quality.

To say that this area is commonly ignored is to understate the case. Many organisations do not have quality requirements for their own data, let alone be able to supply them to a third party. Yet without such quality requirements, the third party is not only not bound to supply quality data to the recipient, but does not even know what quality is required.

Responsibilities of the Receiver

It is unfortunately not enough to simply write requirements for effective data management into a contract and then sit back and assume that all will be well. The recipient organisation needs to ensure that the supplier has the best opportunity to meet expectations. It needs to actively manage the contract, the data and the supplier itself. The recipient organisation has four major responsibilities:

Discuss expectations

Everything is easier if planned in advance, and data supply is no different. The organisation should understand the supplier's expectations of what they will provide in detail. It needs to see how the supplier intends to conform to the organisation's expectations of the data.

Often it is relatively easy for the supplier to build-in quality early in the process, so quality is an inherent part of the solution. On the other hand it may be very hard to retro-fit it in later.

Include Data Management in Contract

This may appear an obvious statement but its surprising how many contracts for supply of third party data entirely exclude details of the data, how it will be managed, and especially its quality.

One organisation I worked with frankly admitted that none of their contracts for supply of data included a detailed requirement for data quality.

Make it Easy As Possible

It is a responsibility of the recipient to make it as easy as possible for the supplier to comply with the data management of the recipient organisation. This includes:

- Supply of data model
- Supply of hierarchies
- Supply of data requirements and especially data quality requirements
- Supply of data standards

It also helps to explain why you need quality data, and the downstream effect on your organisation. People will be more receptive if they can see a real business reason for what appears at first sight to be a spurious request.

Check Data Received

Finally, it is the job of the recipient to act to ensure that the supplier is meeting contractual obligations. I mentioned above the manufacturing shop that carefully checked received parts to ensure they met requirements. All of this due diligence ensured that any subsequent product was fit for purpose. A information recipient should do the same. This may include:

- Examination of received data. It might appear obvious, but almost no organisations check the quality of data received on a regular basis. Profile the incoming data, or define key metrics that will inform you of the quality. Note that a checksum does not guarantee data quality, it only guarantees that the data is received in the same state that it is transmitted. Rubbish correctly transmitted is still rubbish.
- Reporting on received data. Let people know what you are receiving, and let the supplier know that you are reporting on their data.
- Internal audit of the supplier. If the supplier is providing information that is critical to your organisation then it is entirely reasonable for internal audit to visit that organisation and ensure that it is not exposing the organisation to undue risk.

To achieve the above, a little more investment is required than is usually undertaken by both the third party and the receiving organisation.

In addition, many third parties appear to be uninterested in actively working with their customers on data and data quality. The receiving organisation is expected to take the information as-is and not ask awkward questions. This causes frustration and ultimately contractual disputes that should be easily avoided. Given in many outsource agreements the monies and effort on both sides are significant, it appears surprising that collaborative data management appears rarely attempted, let alone successfully achieved.

However, at the crux, it is in the recipient's interest to give the best possible chance for good data to be supplied by the third party - given the effect of poor data will be on their business. It is their decisions that will be poor, their marketing that will be misaligned, their customer that will be dissatisfied, and the reputational damage will rebound on them, and the regulator is unlikely to accept "but it wasn't our fault" as an acceptable excuse.

Summary

More and more organisations are outsourcing some elements of information production. This means that corporate information quality is now dependent on a third party outside your control. These risks need to be mitigated, transferred, or avoided. How is this done? The data architect, being responsible for data flow, must be aware of these risks and act to manage them.

The approach is through holding a third party to the same data standards as the organisation holds itself, and metaphorically x-raying, measuring and checking that the data arrives is to specification. Ensuring this is done is one of the many responsibilities – and challenges - for the data architect.

Chapter 17: Data Modelling

Introduction

I mentioned at the start of the book that data architecture did not equal data modelling and that equating the two did a disservice to both. That said, an understanding of data modelling is essential knowledge for any data architect. As such, this chapter looks to introduce the concepts of data modelling, and delve a little deeper.

Like other chapters, but especially this one, I would strongly recommend further reading as data modelling is as much an art form as a knowledge base.

> *"A frequently overlooked aspect of data quality management is that of data model quality. We often build data models quickly, in the midst of a development project, and with the singular goal of database design. Yet the implications of those models are far reaching and long-lasting. They affect the structure of implemented data, the ability to adapt to change, understanding of and communication about data, definition of data quality rules, and much more. In many ways, high quality data begins with high quality data models."*
>
> Steve Hoberman, Data Modeling Made Simple: A Practical Guide for Business and IT Professionals, Technics Publications, 2005.

What is Data Modelling?

Data modelling is the micro-architecture of data. Architecture at the field level rather than architecture at the database or project or enterprise level. That said the scope of a data model can vary from just the data required for a project or use case, or the data across the whole enterprise.

But what is data modelling?

The best definition I can come up with is that data modelling is the process of designing data structures so they best fit their use. Different structures are applicable for different uses. So if the use is to create lists of customer transactions then the data needs to be structured in the best way to do this efficiently. If the use is to be able to search customer accounts then the structure may differ. The use of the data will determine which is the best design for the data at the micro scale.

I have mentioned before that there is a fundamental difference between the data structure good for writing data, and the data structure good for reading data for business use. They are usually polar opposites. Traditional data warehouses are generally optimised for efficient write, and try and only store every item of data once. However this is very inefficient for reporting.

Example

A list of all the invoices ever issued by a company with their issue dates may be efficient storage, but its annoying if you only want invoices for the last month. To report on the total of last month, the database engine would have to search through ALL invoices in the table and pick the ones that were issued in the last month by calculating "present date - invoice date" in every case. Or, if the database had a "month of issue" field, it could just use that. Of course that would be duplicating data, but it makes the query work faster.

So what does data modelling involve?

- The ability to understand business requirements in terms of the data structures that will be needed to support them.
- The ability to design and document those structures.
- Plus the ability to understand business meaning and interpret this into data structures.

Why is Data Modelling Important?

Primarily, performance and efficiency. Both of which translate into cost and user satisfaction. In this chapter I will cover traditional "relational" data modelling, and then discuss the options available when it comes to NoSQL data modelling.

First, however, I will discuss the corporate data model.

The Corporate Data Model

It is often suggested that the nirvana of data modelling is to have a corporate data model that covers every attribute in the enterprise. All databases are then constructed with the same structure, with the same attributes, having the same meaning. But is this a realistic goal for the organisation?

In my view the answer is no, a corporate data model is not a realistic goal, unless it is a conceptual/logical model at a very high level. I do not think it is possible to have a detailed attribute-level corporate data model. This view comes from practical observation of watching attempts to build one in most organisations I have worked.

So why doesn't it work? There are a number of reasons:

- It takes a very long time to create a data model. In a large organisation it may take years to model every single attribute in the organisation. How many attributes are we talking about? A core system can easily contain 20,000-50,000 attributes. Creating a comprehensive data model can take years.

- Data models need to be different depending on the use case. A data model for a warehouse will need to be different from a data consumption layer. Forcing every part of the organisation into using the same model is going to cause performance issues.

- Stability is an issue. For a corporate data model to be useable then it needs to stop changing, and realistically, and practically, organisations change all the time. New data is ingested, new products developed. Keeping a corporate data model up to date can be a full time job for many people. Then who retrofits the new data model into the databases which have already been built? Do they all have to wait for the new data model to be finished before they can onboard the latest product? Businesses don't work like that.

- As soon as an organisation outsources any part of its data to a third party, or buys a third party application, then the system breaks. Third parties will have their own data models and will not rebuild their applications for a single organisation, however large. So the instant a third party system is used either the enterprise data model has to be rebuilt, or extended, or simply abandoned.

Notwithstanding the above, *project* data modelling absolutely needs to be performed at the detail level, and linked to the use case it supports. Therefore the ideal arrangement is a high level corporate data model at the conceptual/logical level, and a physical data model at the project level that is consistent with the higher level enterprise one, but includes greater detail.

Traditional Data Modelling

Types of Data Model

There are three types of data model in a traditional data modelling environment:

- Conceptual data models are high level models of the area of interest (the relevant domain). They are in business language.
- Logical data models are more technical, and describe the detailed solution one level down from the conceptual model.
- Physical data models show the detailed field-by-field relationships and names and are specific to the implementation.

Conceptual Data Model

At its highest level, a conceptual data model may consist of nothing more than what is called an entity relationship diagram.

This example, with two entities (customer and product), reads from left to right and right to left respectively:

"Each customer may have one or many products: Each product may have one or many customers."

This (which is a many to many relationship, in traditional databases these are to be avoided) is not very helpful from a database design point of view. As a result, a better modelling solution may be:

This reads (left hand side): "Each customer may have one or many accounts; each account must have one and only one customer."

The right hand side reads: "Each account must have one and only one product; each product may have one or many accounts."

Given this information we can then start building this out into more detail. Here I will concentrate on "customer" and ignore the account and product area from now on to keep matters simple.

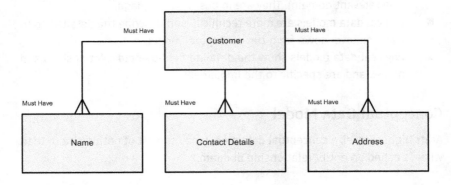

It is worth noting that we are trying to avoid many-to-many relationships. In a relational database many-to-many relationships cause problems across the whole range of database operations. Hence it is normal practice to "break" a many-to-many relationship with a bridging table.

Logical Data Model

Looking at the wording used when discussing the conceptual data model, it is noticeable that we are entirely dealing here with abstract concepts of entities that are related. To move to a logical model, we start moving down into the next level when talking about the attributes each entity may have.

For example, name may have components such as:

- Title
- Forename
- Middle Name
- Surname
- Post-nominal abbreviations

A logical data model may also incorporate business rules, for example how a product is described. If a data model is used consistency across an organisation then problems relating to incompatibility of data from different systems will be significantly reduced. This will lead to;

- reduced operating costs
- reduced implementation costs
- greater clarity of information
- significantly reduced interface complexity

A data model is valuable and useful to the organisation. Some organisations (IBM, Teradata and others) can supply data models that will support industry sectors, thus giving an organisation a pre-built solution to which the organisation can align.

Physical Data Model

The last level of data model is the physical. Here we link to the actual database fields. For example:

Table	Field
CusName	CusFirstName
CusName	CusMiddleName
CusName	CusLastName
CusName	CusTitle

Here we have the actual "address" of the data. We can use the above to go and source it.

What's more, if the physical data model in each system is mapped to an organisation-wide logical model, we can relate all information in all systems together.

Non-Relational Data Modelling

As I said earlier, data modelling in a non-relational database can be even more important than in a relational database. Within a NoSQL database the approach is more focused on the overall structure of the database and the data, rather than tables and fields, but the effect is exactly the same as for a relational database.

In a way it is *more* important for NoSQL databases, as whilst many of the decisions in relational databases can be rectified later, many of the same decisions for NoSQL databases cannot be rectified without starting from scratch.

- **Types of database.** The first decision to be taken is what kind of database? Does the use case lend itself towards key-value pairs, document databases, or is the use case more a graph use case, or would wide-column be more appropriate? Whilst most relational databases are similar there is a wide variety between the data structures for NoSQL databases and this can make the difference between the database being a very good fit for the use case, or a very bad one.

- **Vendor and capability.** Once the organisation has decided on a type of database (key-value, etc), the next decision is vendor. Each vendor has their own flavour of NoSQL database and each database has different capabilities. As such, the database designer has to make the decision between which capabilities are essential for meeting the use case, which are nice to have, and which are unnecessary.

- **What kind of data?** Whilst NoSQL databases can often support a very wide range of data, the wider the range of data the potentially slower the performance. Does the designer want to limit the types of data, and if so, to what? The wider the range, the higher the overhead put on the database.

- **What will the document include?** Whilst the document model may be infinitely variable, how will it be structured for the best performance? Are there certain types of data that should not be allowed?

- **Indexes and keys.** A critical decision for NoSQL databases is the data to use as index or key. This can make a massive difference to the performance of a database in relation to particular use cases, as indexes make searching on certain data very fast. However if data is not indexed, this may need to be searched line by line. This will be a lot slower than if the data is indexed.

- **Sharding.** Whilst NoSQL databases can scale horizontally, how will this be done. How will the shards interact, where will they be positioned, what data will be held in each? In addition, how will the expansion of the database be managed and how will this affect the data?

- **ACID transactions?** Does the use case require ACID transactions? There are some NoSQL databases that do support ACID transactions to a limited extent. What is required, and how does this affect the use case?

- **Partitioning.** Partitioning is key for NoSQL databases. In fairness it is also key for relational databases too. How will partitions be managed, on what basis will the databases be split, and what effect will this have on the performance? For example, a common way of partitioning is to split by date, so that reports on the current year can be created quickly as they only have to look at the "current year" partition. However multi-year reports showing progress over time can, as a result, take ages as every partition would need to be queried.

In short, with NoSQL databases there are many key design decisions that need to be taken up front. Although some of those decisions on structure are common with relational databases many are unique to NoSQL databases, and cannot be rectified later without a lot of work if the wrong decision is taken.

Of course, all of the above needs to be related to the business use. Every key decision must include the needs of the business users. What are the data requirements, and what kind of data will the consumers need? What kind of data will they need fast, what kind of data can they wait for?

Summary

Data modelling is data architecture at the micro level. It bridges the gap between business understanding and the "technical address" of the data. It also organizes and structures the data in a way that supports the requirements of the organisation.

Data modelling is critical to get right. If an organisation has 1000 systems and they each structure their data in a different way then creating a consistent view of the organisation for management or a regulator will become practically impossible. Data modelling choices can have significant impact on what is and is not possible with information.

In short, data modelling should be done well.

SECTION 3: Implementation

- Principles of Data Architecture

- Example architectures

- Pain points and how to solve them

- Designing architectural change

- Implementing architectural change

Chapter 18: Section Introduction

This third and final section of the book looks to take the knowledge built up in the previous two sections and apply it in practice. This section looks at data architecture design more holistically, bringing together the various architectural building blocks into end-to-end architectures.

We start the section with data architectural principles - what are the key boundaries within which the data architect should work?

We follow with a description of the typical data architecture pain points within organisations, with explanation of why they are a problem, and also how to identify them.

Next we will cover example architectures. These are real life "good" architectures than can be used as patterns for reuse. The advantages and disadvantages of each will be discussed.

Next we cover how "bad" architectures can be transformed into "good" ones - what are the real-life changes within data architectures that can make things better?

Lastly we discuss the implementation of architectural change. This is of necessity a small subset of the total subject, as every organisation is different and its capacity and method for change varies. I will look at some of the architectural change frameworks, and give an example of how these could be implemented in practice.

Chapter 19: Data Architecture Principles

Introduction

If we consider that data architecture is the design of data flow in an organisation, then we need to talk about what is - and is not - good design. All forms of design have "best practice", the accepted industry wisdom of the way design should be done. Best practice is commonly rooted in the accumulated mistakes of decades. It is, if you like, case law for information systems.

It is impossible for the Data Architect to be everywhere all the time, and the creation of design principles sets what is - and is not - acceptable. This clear statement of clarity and direction is essential. It is also essential to cascade these principles into the organisation so that all architects are aware of the right thing to do.

This chapter contains a set of data architecture principles that embody best data architecture practice. There is no particular "order" to the below principles. They all need to be considered and followed in order to make the most out of data in the organisation.

The Zeroth Principle.

Before we start, there is, however, a "zeroth" principle, and that is that data architecture, as a practice, should be respected. This may appear a strange principle, but I believe it is key.

Often, a lack of understanding prompts both business and IT to believe that data architecture is an "optional" specialism that is not needed. This is in stark contrast to, for example, data security. If a data security expert tells a project not to do something, then, generally, they don't. However data architecture principles are ignored within many organisations when time is tight, or budget is short.

This should not occur. The natural result of such decisions is this brings risk and cost to the organisation in exactly the same way as data security failings. Over time, the costs to the organisation spiral out of control, the organisation becomes uncompetitive and faces an inability to change. It also makes incorrect decisions on poor data and may result in regulatory fines.

Data Architects should be respected and the principles of best practice applied to change within the organisation. Again, if the statement was "best principles of data security should be applied within an organisation" no-one would have any issue. The same should apply to data architecture.

Principle 1: Clear Strategy and Direction

A summary would be: **"we need to know where we are going**."

Anyone who is creating data flows should have a clear idea of good practice. The organisation must have a defined data architecture strategy, direction and guidelines. No part of the organisation should be in any doubt of what is the right thing to do.

This strategy needs to be communicated. A strategy that is only seen by senior execs does not help the project managers and architects on the ground who are trying to implement new capabilities. So, after strategy is created, then it needs to be rolled out, and governance put in place to ensure that deviations from strategy are detected.

Principle 2: Data Standards in Place

The summary here is **"guardrails and best practice**."

Key to ensuring that an organisation develops good data architecture is having standards in place that ensure best practice is clearly communicated across the organisation.

These standards include, but are not limited to:

- Architecture patterns
- Modelling standards
- The existence of a data model

- Architecture documentation standards
- Approval and escalation guidelines
- Control standards
- Evidence standards
- Tooling standards
- Governance standards

In short, the organisation needs to clearly state what is acceptable and right, and what is unacceptable and wrong. Whilst it is accepted that due to timing pressures or budget pressures the ideal outcome may not always be possible, there must be a process to ensure that any deviations from best practice are approved.

It is very common for data architecture professionals to be pressured into accepting poor data architecture by the business or IT. It is the role of the Data Architect to try and make both sides understand that poor architecture has negative effects, both in the short and the long term.

Data standards allow the Data Architect to have a baselined, documented standard to point to and say "no, this is best practice, which is there for the good of the organisation, and if you wish to go against best practice, then there are standards for this too."

In short, data standards are the "constitution" of data in the organisation.

Principle 3: Simplicity

The summary of this principle is "**complexity breeds risk**."

The more complicated a data architecture, then the more likely it is to go wrong, the more difficult it will be to change, and the more difficult to identify errors.

Therefore, when designing a solution, or, as an Enterprise Data Architect designing the data flows throughout an organisation, the rule should be "as simple as possible." This means minimise the number of warehouses, minimise the number of interfaces, and especially minimise the number of transformations. Every single one is a potential failure point.

If you have to have a system with thousands of feeds, make sure that the control mechanism around it is designed to cope safely with that number.

If you can, keep it simple.

Principle 4: Data is Accessible

The summary here is "**we need to be able to find and use data.**"

We have mentioned in a prior chapter that many fulfillment systems have back end databases storing data that is not immediately accessible to the organisation. Many businesses face challenges as this data is "locked in" these back end databases and is never propagated downstream into warehouses where the data can be used for reporting, management information and analytics.

Almost all data a business creates is useful in some way. Analytics tools can be used to draw conclusions that will help the business and/or its customers. Often the data that allows the organisation to draw such conclusions isn't obvious at first, but arrived at by experimentation, looking for correlation between seemingly disparate fields.

Therefore any data store must be designed with the ability to share its data. Ideally, the default design should share data into a data warehouse or marketplace of some kind where others parts of the organisation can access it.

In short, "don't build data silos."

Principle 5: Appropriate Data Sourcing

The summary of this principle would be "**get data from the right place.**"

It doesn't matter whether the data is customer data, reference data, product data or transactional data, there will always be a right and wrong place to source data.

Let us consider country codes. The most appropriate place to get such reference data is a reference data hub. If all parts of the organisation do this, then when there is a change - for example a new country being formed (e.g. Czech

Republic and Slovakia) then one change in the reference data hub updates everything. Everything from drop-down lists in customer forms to reporting dashboards can change in one go.

If, however, projects are downloading country lists from the Internet and hard coding them into applications, it can be very difficult to create a seamless data flow. Transactions may simply "disappear" as the source system contains the correct country but downstream systems don't. This may very literally cost millions.

A second example is for data that needs to be widely distributed across the organisation, e.g. transaction data. In theory core systems should propagate data to an agreed consumption point. Core systems shouldn't be used as the consumption point themselves as this will increase the load on those systems and potentially impact their ability to do what they are supposed to do – serve the needs of customers. So the core systems may feed data downstream to a single place that is the consumption point. That consumption point can then implement data governance to ensure that only entitled consumers will get it, and that the data is appropriate quality, integrity, etc.

Unfortunately for many organisations it is much easier to get data from the wrong place than the right one. It is easier to go to core systems directly, it is easier to download off the Internet. The result is data quality will suffer, and the organisation will make the wrong decisions on the wrong data.

Principle 6: Transparent Data Transformation

The summary here is "**you must be able to see how data flows**."

One of the biggest problems that organisations face is that data movement is not transparent. What do I mean by this? Well, in order to properly control the flow of information in an organisation then the organisation needs to know what data is flowing and from where to where.

Unfortunately many systems that transport data are not transparent. Many transport mechanisms include transformation of data. These transformations are often contained in scripts that move and transform data, that may have been written decades ago and never touched since.

So what problems can occur?

A common example is that the formats in the source and target are different. Therefore, when the script was written, the script designer had to make a difficult decision. They didn't have the ability to change either source or target format, so had to fit the source data as best they could.

A particular example from my own experience was mortgage default data. In this case the source system had entries in the "months in arrears" column as NULL (unknown), 0, 1, 2, 3.

Entry	Number of rows
Null	10,000
0	10,000
1	5,000
2	2,000
3	1,000

Using the (dummy) data above, the average months in arrears is 0.66. This is an important metric, as "average months in arrears" is a standard metric for the "health" of the portfolio.

However in the particular real-life example, the target system didn't allow nulls, so all the nulls were transformed into "0." When data was transferred to a downstream systems, this fundamentally changed the perceived risk within that mortgage portfolio, as 10,000 "unknown" values were transformed into the best possible value - "0" - no arrears. Now average months in arrears was 0.43. For someone looking to invest in the portfolio this makes the mortgage portfolio much more attractive. This kind of transformation is very difficult to pick up and almost impossible to find after the event, as it may be buried in millions of lines of code. So data flow must be transparent.

Another example, where a transformation should happen but doesn't, is dates. Imagine the source system is a proprietary system by an American software house and uses American date format. The target system may use the usual date format in the rest of the world. Obviously the script that moves the data from one system to the other should transform the data.

If it doesn't, and simply drops data that will not fit in the target database, then whilst 1/1/1970 will transfer correctly, 2/3/1970 will be reversed (from Feb 3rd to 2nd March) and 14/4/1970 may simply be dropped, losing the organisational data.

It is essential for sustainable data architecture that data transformations are documented and available. In order to manage and control what is going on, then you need to know what is going on, and if you don't know what is going on, you're not in control.

Principle 7: Maintain Data Lineage

The summary here is "**the organisation needs to know where its data comes from**"

An organisation needs to understand its data lineage – what data flows from where to where. Why is this important? Because in order to know that the data it is making decisions on is correct – and therefore the decisions are correct and justified – the organisation needs to know where its data has come from. Did it come from a trusted source, did it come from a spreadsheet on someone's desktop. Did it flow through well controlled systems, or a series of random fileshares where anyone could modify the data?

How lineage is documented can vary – automatic tools can provide some cover, but many organisations perform this job by manual mapping. This can be challenging if the source and target are not clearly understood. If, for example a ETL program maps "col 1" to "Cus1" then there's not real automatic way to understand what data is flowing and why. Manual investigation will be required.

Poor understanding and documentation of data lineage affects the whole organisation. I have mentioned decisions, but lack of data lineage also makes it impossible to address data quality problems. It is difficult to ensure that data is being sourced from the correct location, and it is likely that regulatory and legal issues will also occur. For example, how can you ensure that you are not breaking data sharing regulations across borders if you don't know where the data in the database is coming from?

In short, data lineage is about tracking data through the organisation, so you know where it is going, and where it has come from.

Principle 8: Maintain Quality

The summary here is "**maintain quality at the highest level possible**."

If we consider that the job of the Data Architect is to get the right data to the right place at the right time so the right people can make the right decisions, the key here is "right data." If it is the wrong data than the wrong decisions will be taken.

Best practice states that by far the cheapest way of attaining data quality is to capture data right first time. This is much cheaper than trying to clean it up later.

1-10-100 Rule

A commonly accepted rule within the data quality profession is the 1-10-100 rule. This states that:

- Getting data right first time costs £1.
- The effort to correct if it starts out wrong is ten times that - £10.
- If it is never corrected, then it costs ten times that again -£100, as the effect of the mistake occur time and time again.

Obviously it goes without saying that if data is captured at good quality that quality should be maintained through the organisation. Intermediate processes between source and consumption should not corrupt the data. If data is changed or corrupted there is often no way to get back to the original and therefore no way of knowing if the data under consideration is actually "right" or "wrong."

I would take this further and say that the above is applicable even if the data is incorrect, because as soon as data is corrected "in-flight" it removes the opportunity to correct the root cause of the issue. For example, if a date is seen as "12/17/2023" (December 17th 2023) then clearly that's an American date format. Depending on country, this points to an error in source systems or data entry, and potentially in poor validation processes. Knowing this, the organisation can put in process a remediation exercise that will not only solve this particular entry, but will correct the systematic error that allowed it to occur in the first place.

However if data is automatically translated into normal format by an automatic process, then the opportunity to correct the root cause of the problem is lost.

In addition, by masking obvious errors, then discovery of un-obvious errors is lost. To use the same example, if a system is also creating a date of 03/02/2023 is this 3rd February or 2nd of March? We don't know. If it's a customer date of birth and hence a security question its really important to know the right answer.

There are arguments both ways. Implementing automatic remediation at exit from the source system cleanses data for all downstream users. But, knowing there are errors allows them to be addressed. Therefore maintaining poor quality data - until it needs to be used at which point it can be cleansed and cleansed *once* - has value too.

In short. Get data right first time. Once it starts off wrong, it can be difficult and expensive to fix.

Principle 9: Use the Right Tools

The summary of this principle is "**use the right data construct for the requirements at hand**."

A good example of this is a common challenge around operational and non-operational systems.

Operational systems – and by this I mean fulfillment systems – the "core systems" of the organisation – are critical to its operation. Significant investment is made in the hardware and software to ensure resiliency. Systems are backed up regularly, and may even run with backup systems "ready to go" in a hot/hot setup where there are actually two, geographically separated core systems, both of which are up to date and ready to take over the whole company if required.

All of this resilience comes at a price, and that price can be very steep.

On the other hand, reporting systems are generally not that critical. If a business doesn't get a daily report the world won't end. If a data warehouse has to wait two days to get an update, the business will survive. Yes, many business users may complain, but the organisation will not collapse.

The investment in resiliency is therefore much lower.

A key principle of data architecture is to not make operational systems dependent on reporting systems. This is often termed as "operationalising the warehouse." A typical example is where data is held in the warehouse without which the operational systems cannot function. Country codes, for example. This kind of poor design means that either the organisation has to accept increased risk – or has to spend vast amounts of money ensuring the warehouse is a resilient as operational systems.

It is best practice to keep the systems separate. In the wider view, the principle is to make sure you use the right tool, in the right architectural location, for the requirements.

In short. Right tool for right job.

Principle 10: Minimise Duplication

The summary here is "**don't pay for the same thing twice**"

This principle is concerned with several parts of data architecture. An example is data tooling. In any large organisation, control of data tooling is often a struggle. Different parts of an organisation may pay for different tools to do the same job. In addition, new products come on the market constantly, and if an organisation samples them all they will soon have organisational chaos.

For *each capability*, each organisation should generally have *one* tool. This tool should be under governance.

Without this principle the organisation will:

■   Pay excessive license fees

- Have a skills issue – staff in one part of the organisation will be unable to transfer between departments as they will be skilled on a different tool
- Be locked into proprietary data formats and unable to share information across the organisation
- Lack agility

In a large organisation with many silos this is very difficult to do, as holistic knowledge of implementations in different areas of the organisation is difficult to achieve. A strong tooling governance function is key. For the data architect, the job is to discover what is being used, and reuse, rather than replicate.

The same applies to larger data architecture constructs. Unless there is good reason, it is poor practice to build duplicative systems - for example multiple data warehouses.

In short, do it once, do it well.

Summary

It is essential that data architecture has clear principles. These principles allow data architecture as a function to set clear guidelines on best practice that can be used to inform themselves and the rest of the organisation on what is right, and what is wrong.

Data architecture principles create a constitution for data design in the organisation. They can be used to ensure that what is developed will best support the organisation and its data strategy.

In this chapter I have outlined a set of principles. This set is not exhaustive, and many additional principles can be created. What works for the individual organisation is the decision for the Data Architect.

Chapter 20: Example Architectures

Introduction

At this point of the book, the reader should have a clear understanding of the basic data architecture building blocks. They should understand the responsibilities and roles of the Data Architect, and understand the principles of best practice that can be used to ensure good data flow through an organisation.

The aim of this chapter is to bring this knowledge together and give practical examples of the way systems are linked together in real organisations. This gives a reader knowledge of architectures they may experience in real life.

All of the examples used are real examples. For each I have given a high level description and a brief summary of advantages and disadvantages.

Example 1: Simple System

We will start with a very simple system and then build up the complexity.

The simplest system is a channel application with a back end database. The channel application – for example a fulfillment system – takes data from customers (orders, personal details, etc) and saves them to a database. The same database is then used for business reporting.

The advantage here is that data will always be up to date. The reporting will always be exactly in sync with the actual operations of the business. There is also a simplicity to the system – minimal data transfers reduces the risk of data transfer errors.

The disadvantage is performance and risk. Using the same database for both write (from the channel application) and read (from the reporting application) will compromise performance. It also introduces risk, that mis-configured reporting will bring the database down, in which case the channel application is effectively down too, and the users are presented with errors on trying to conduct business – not a good look.

Also, the database will grow over time, and performance will get slower over time. The best solution here is to separate the reporting workload and the data it uses from the day to day operations of the organisation.

Example 2: Add a Warehouse

So we add a warehouse. This not only separates the workload, but also provides a location where years of historical data can be safely stored without interfering with the channel application. The data can be offloaded daily, resulting in a complete historical record, but also a fast operational back end.

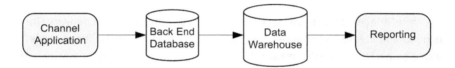

This also allows the organisation to amalgamate the data from many systems in one place. So, for example, if you want a view of what customers are doing across all products, then this works. The data warehouse can take many feeds from many operational systems and amalgamate them into a holistic view of the organisation.

The disadvantage is that this architecture may introduce delay. If the transfer from the back end database is end of day, then the data in the warehouse is 24 hours out of date. So the architect needs to think about whether this will meet business requirements, and if not, can the transfer mechanism be modified to, for example, microbatch?

An additional challenge here is that what do you optimise the warehouse for? Do you optimise for write (for minimal impact on the back end) or read (for best performance reporting)? Given a choice, it is better to optimise the warehouse for write, as this minimises the load on the critical front end systems.

However the impact is on reporting. This is less critical than the channel application, but is still not ideal. There isn't a good solution. So we need something better.

Example 3: Add a Datamart

We can solve the above problem of the warehouse not being good for reporting by adding a datamart. Here a channel application has a back end database where it stores all its transactions. It offloads the day's transactions to a data warehouse at the end of each day. The data warehouse then offloads to a datamart which is structured for reporting, and then there is a reporting layer at the end.

So, let us analyse this simple system. It separates reporting from delivery. This is good and means the channel application and its back end database are left alone to perform the important role of running the day to day operations of the organisation. The warehouse aggregates historical data, and data from all departments across the organisation. The datamart structures the data for fast reporting. All good so far.

However this architecture also brings disadvantages. One of the big problems is timing. If the batch process to the data warehouse is end of day, and the movement to the datamart is also end of day, then the reporting is T+2 days. This is a significant lag, and it would be necessary to check with the business users of the reporting whether this was appropriate.

What are the options if it were not appropriate? There are several:

- The batch process sending data to the datamart could run immediately after the process that placed data in the data warehouse. This reduces the time lag to T+1.
- The back end database could use microbatch or CDC to put data in the warehouse, and the same could be used to put data into the datamart. This allows near real time reporting.

- We could use an ODS (see next example).

Another problem here is transformations. There will be transformations from the back end database to the warehouse. There will also be transformations from the warehouse to the datamart. We now need to manage those transformations as we have introduced transformation risk. We are also increasing the number of "hops" the data takes. We are introducing complexity. With complexity brings risk.

Example 4: Operational Data Store (ODS)

We mentioned above that one big problem with the above architecture is timing. For many organisations a key business requirement is timely reporting. The business needs to know if there is a problem earlier than T+2. One option is changing the method of transfer, but this can be expensive. Another option is adding an Operational Data Store (an ODS).

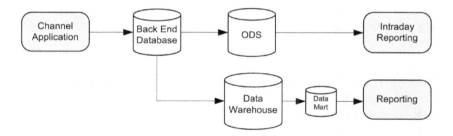

An ODS is a repository used for short term reporting. The back end database offloads to an ODS on a microbatch basis (say once every 15 mins) as well as to the data warehouse. The ODS provides timely reporting, and the data warehouse provides longer term reporting.

In this architecture the time-critical operational reporting could be done from the ODS and then the data warehouse would only be used for month end and historical reporting. The ODS typically only contains limited data history - typically the last months' data. After that the data is available in the warehouse. The ODS is cleared on a monthly basis. Keeping the ODS small and limiting its data history keeps the reporting performance high.

Have we now solved all our problems?

We still have the problem with the transformations but in a different way. There will be transformations from the back end database to the ODS and also to the warehouse. There will also be transformations from the warehouse to the mart. Therefore one risk is that the intraday reporting and the longer term reporting will not be consistent. This could be solved by routing the data from the ODS to the warehouse as below. This also has the advantage that the critical channel application only has to send data to one downstream target, reducing load on that critical system.

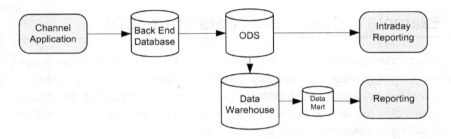

We have also added more complexity, and we know that for every additional data transfer we increase the risk of data going wrong.

However, the above example – warehouse + ODS + datamart – is a very good balancing act between complexity (and hence risk) and meeting business requirements. It has been a standard pattern for traditional data architectures for many years and it is effective. A Data Architect will encounter this pattern many times in real organisations.

Example 5: Application Programming Interfaces (APIs)

We will now change direction slightly, and look at more modern architectures. The above pattern has been effective. However it has come under increasing pressure in several key areas as organisations have modernised.

- The movement to 24/7 operations meant that the window for an end-of-day transfer from channel applications ceased to exist.
- Business users wanted real time data on demand. A business user needed to see a sale on reporting systems instantly. Partly because of the need to make quick decisions, but also the sale data fed into

procurement and shipping systems. The rise of same-day or next-day delivery meant waiting a day to know about sales was time the business simply didn't have.

- Customers wanted real time data on demand too. A customer who makes an order wants to see that order, on their smartphone, instantly. They do not want to wait even five minutes.
- Organisations had built many thousands of data feeds from source systems to a warehouse, and then more feeds from warehouses to consumption systems. In many cases the feeds were undocumented. Understanding of lineage had been lost. The complexity risk was getting out of hand.

There needed to be a better way that would solve for the above problems. The solution was Application Programming Interfaces (APIs). This is a very different architecture..

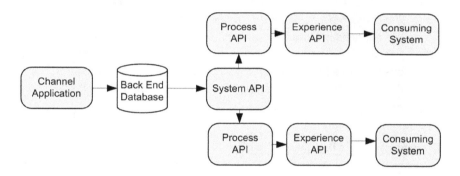

Here the back end database exposes a system API. The system API will transfer data – on demand – to any downstream consumer authorised to request data. The nature of the data transfer is variable – which is a big change from the "fixed" transfers in previous examples. Provided the right fields are populated, the API can change the data that is included as the "payload."

The system API is in turn "called" by process APIs which may amalgamate the results from many system APIs from many systems to create a dataset. This is in the same way as a data warehouse may combine data from many systems, but it is done "on the fly." There is no data storage.

This dataset may need to be presented differently depending on the consumer – so display on a customer smartphone may require a different format to business reporting, but based on the same data. Therefore Experience APIs will take the data that is created by the Process API and format it for the channel in question.

But this brings its own problems, in that we again have load on the back end database. However this load is reduced by the use of a standard format. The load - and hence risk of overloading the back end database - can be also lowered by using a cache (see next example).

I should note, by the way, that the above is simplified. The API ecosystem will generally include an API gateway which handles authorisation – so that not just anyone can request data – and the ecosystem can also handle load balancing on the back end system.

The API architecture is flexible and solves for a lot of the problems with the traditional architectures. It does however have two drawbacks.

- The consuming system has to request the data. What if something critical happens in between requests? How often does it request the data?
- Not all of the data is interesting. Most data is pretty routine. In reality business need to primarily know only about events they need to make decisions about. How do you filter the interesting from the mass of routine?

Example 6: Using a Cache

I mentioned above that if you wish to lower the load on the back end system then it is possible to use a cache. What's a cache?

A cache is a data store that exists to hold an identical replica of another data store for any reason. It is a proxy for the source data store and acts in its stead. Typical reasons for caches include:

- The source database is suffering from high load, so the data is off-loaded once, and then all subsequent reads are from the cache. This leaves the source database to get on with its job. In this case the cache is operating exactly as an ODS.
- The source database is geographically separated from the consumption. Pushing data over a large geographical distance may introduce delays that are unacceptable for consumers. So the cache holds data nearer to

the point of consumption so that data can be retrieved quickly.

- Many databases hold some data that both changes quickly (e.g. account balance), and also data that changes slowly, or not at all. A cache can hold that data that moves slowly or not at all (customer DOB, for example). That reduces load on the source system, as only the fast moving data needs to be retrieved, and the slow moving data can be obtained from the cache.

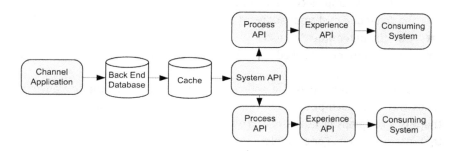

In the above example, the cache is reducing load on the source system. If the cache is a replica of the source (for example using database replication or change data capture) then it should always be only a few seconds behind the back end in terms of data.

Using this architecture allows the users get both up to date data, and the source system is isolated.

Example 7: Streaming

If APIs are one way of getting around the problems of a traditional architecture, another is streaming. Streaming architectures, as well as solving the problems with traditional architectures, also look to solve the two problems mentioned above as drawbacks of API architectures.

- The provision of real time data as it happens without a consumer having to specifically request it.
- Not all data is interesting to the downstream consumer.

Streaming uses the concept of "events." An "event" may be a customer order, or a change in customer details, or a payment – anything really. Logic is built into the source system or its back end database identifying events that are interesting to downstream consumers.

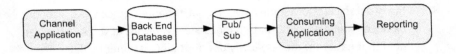

The back end system (or cache/ODS as a proxy) will "publish" the "event" whenever it occurs. The publication will be to a stream of data that contains similar events. Examples could include:

- a "changed customer address" stream
- a "customer order" stream
- a "customer has backed out of the transaction at the last stage" stream

Key to this architecture is the source system doesn't care whether anyone reads the data. Each published event is a message that is sent out whether there is a recipient or not. It is up to the consumer to connect to the stream that interests them. For example:

- The dispatch department that puts together customer orders can subscribe to the "orders" and "change of address" stream, but doesn't really care about the "payment" stream.
- The application that is putting together the end of day financial data certainly won't care about customer address, but will care about transactions and payments.
- The marketing department will care about the "customer has backed out of the transaction at the last stage" stream. They will want to know why. Has the customer changed their mind? Can the sale be salvaged by contacting the customer directly?

Each stream of events is not necessarily recorded. The streaming engine (Pub/Sub in the diagram above) will normally hold a short term - typically 24 hours - copy of events in case of failure or downtime. However, any authorised consumer can subscribe to any stream and then save it into their own database. The data warehouse can still be the data warehouse with its years of history, it just receives the data in very small chunks.

The use of streaming architecture allows consumers to narrow their focus to what interests them, rather than having to obtain a full data extract and then work it out. It also reduces load on the source system, as it only has to emit data when "interesting" events occur.

This disadvantages of event streaming are:

- Cost of implementation - streaming requires changes to the source system which may be difficult or expensive, or both, especially if the source system is old.
- Ordering. Which event came first? This is not always clear. However it is possible to get around this by timestamps or event numbering.

However, event streaming is currently one of the most promising architectures to solve the challenges with legacy architectures.

The last three examples I will give are "variations on a theme." They are specific variations to the traditional architecture that the data architect may see in real-life organisations. I have mentioned all three previously in the book, and therefore it makes sense to demonstrate how they would work in practice.

Example 8: Data Lake (ELT)

I covered the concept of data lakes in an earlier chapter. As stated then the data lake tries to reduce some of the heavy lifting in getting data into data warehouses. The challenge the data lake tries to overcome is that, for a warehouse architecture, data has to be transformed before it lands in the warehouse.

This applies whether – or not – the data is subsequently used. Given the transformation is computationally expensive, this is not ideal. In addition, the transformation takes time and effort on the part of business and IT to set up, so again, introduces a lot of work potentially wasted.

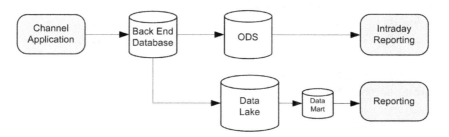

For the data lake an ELT pattern is used. Extract and load as-is into the lake, and then only data needed is further transformed into marts. The effect here is to speed implementation time and reduce complexity and improve lineage understanding and clarity.

In terms of the overall architecture it is mostly identical to a warehouse architecture with the same advantages and disadvantages. A significant change though is that a data lake is designed to accept almost any kind of data. A warehouse is traditionally tightly constrained. So a lake can accept traditional text data, but also pictures, videos, or streaming data in a much more flexible way than a warehouse.

Example 9: Cloud Solutions (GCP)

The next example I'll cover uses Google Cloud Platform. Strictly speaking the architecture is not significantly different by using public cloud, in the sense that the general flow of data is very similar to exactly the same thing on premises.

There are a lot of misconceptions around cloud hosted data architectures and I therefore wanted to bring in an example here. I will use GCP for this example, but a very similar architecture would be used for any of the other cloud providers. The names of the applications would be different, but the architecture would be similar.

The start point is the same, in that data starts at an on-prem core system. However this core system outputs data to a cloud project. Within the cloud project there is something called "cloud storage." This is simply a storage location – a bit like a hard drive – where a file – in this case a file containing data – can be saved. The file in cloud storage is then "read" into a product called "Big Query" – which is Google's superscale data warehouse. At this point the dataset becomes available for querying. However Big Query creates an output which is not overly user-friendly, so the visualisation is created by another product "Data Studio", which reads from the datasets created in big query.

Using the above architecture introduces benefits regarding scalability and resiliency, and may being benefit to cost, but if the data is transmitted at the end of the working day, the problems we have discussed around time delay will still apply.

The point I would like to stress is any of the architectures I have discussed in this chapter can be implemented on cloud. There are significant advantages as a result, but use of cloud does not solve basic data architecture challenges. It does however give the architect access to a wide variety of toolsets all of which are designed to be integrated and implemented quickly and scalably.

Example 10: Third Party Provider

The last example introduces the concept of outsourcing, discussed at length in a previous chapter. Many organisations outsource a part or a whole of their operations. For example, particular processes – for example accounting – could be outsourced, equally a company may outsource a product to an organisation which specialises in that type of offering.

From a data architecture point of view, the only change is that there needs to be a way of getting the data from the third party into the organisation's systems. In this case an additional component is introduced – that is a concept of a landing pad. The landing pad is essentially a shared space to which both the third party and the consuming organisation have access.

The actual nature of the landing pad can vary. Sometimes it can be a database and the third party has rights to write to the database, sometimes it is a fileshare on a server that can be seen from both directions – either located at the third party or the consumer, and sometimes it is a location on a cloud provider's storage systems.

As per the cloud example, outsourcing to a third party does not solve data architecture problems. It merely puts portions of the overall landscape outside the immediate control of the organisation. This both brings risk, and also adds interfaces to the overall architecture, hence introducing complexity that has to be managed.

Summary

In this chapter I have tried to cover the common data architectures that a Data Architect may encounter in real life organisations. I have covered both traditional architectures and more modern API and streaming architectures.

I should stress that the above are only examples. It is perfectly possible – in fact likely – that most organisations will have many different architectures in play at the same time.

In fact, it is perfectly possible for organisations to have several architectures doing the same thing at the same time. Architectural change is challenging, and situations where a legacy architecture, a current architecture and a future state architecture exist simultaneously within different parts of the organisation are common.

Lastly, I should note that the above are only examples, and examples that are simplified for clarity. Real life architectures may involve much more complexity as data traverses through an organisation. However the basic building blocks will often remain the same.

Chapter 21: Data Architecture Pain Points

Introduction

I mentioned at the end of the previous chapter that a Data Architect may encounter many non-standard architectures in real organisations. The next chapter of the book will cover what might be called "data architecture pain points." The objective is to show examples of where data architecture can go wrong, because sometimes negative examples are good at demonstrating the point. I suspect that to most readers many of these examples will look hauntingly familiar.

This is in no way a comprehensive list of potential issues. It should also be strongly noted that rarely are poor solutions deliberately created. Poor solutions commonly evolve from not enough budget or time. The objective in this chapter is to understand why data architecture issues can occur, what effect it can have, and eventually what can be done, if anything, to fix it. Not to assign blame.

A number of examples have been given. However in this particular area there is little substitute for experience, which is why data architects are essential parts of any organisation.

Example 1: Historical Systems/Applications

Question
Are there any historical systems/applications?

Reason for question and why is this important
- Historical systems are typically of limited capability and difficult to change. As a result there may be any number of "quick fixes" performed in a way that may work, but is not ideal. "Doing it properly" may require significant time and possibly someone who knows prehistoric programming languages. Not doing things properly creates risk. "Bodge jobs"

create risk. Full testing is unlikely to have occurred, and these systems can drop or corrupt data easily, and often do.

- Historical systems do not tend to store modern data well, nor do they lend themselves to easy modification. For example there may not be fields for "email address" or "mobile phone number." Even when the system itself doesn't cause problems, Staff, looking to do their jobs to the best of their ability, may use alternative places to store essential information. Email addresses are commonly just a jumble of words, special characters ("@") and numbers which will not pass validation checks on other fields. The "comments" field may be commonly used to store email addresses, as it is unlikely to have any validation checks.

What can be done?
- Can historical systems be replaced?
- Can governance be put around development on these systems?
- Can the organisation introduce agreed workarounds so that at least everyone is doing the same thing?

Example 2: Siloed Data

Question
Are there many copies of customer data?

Reason for question and why is this important
For data such as critical customer data, the less versions of the truth the better. Ideally there should be a single version of the truth, but many organisations have many customer databases, even if there isn't a 100% overlap. A separate database for each product, for example, is common, and a customer that buys both products is typically recorded separately in each.

The more copies there are, the more confusion around which is correct, and the more they are likely to diverge. In some cases there may be no way to work out which data is correct. In addition, multiple silos mean that every job has to be performed multiple times, ballooning cost of data remediation.

What can be done?
- Collapse the silos. Much easier said than done.
- Ask business owners whether the data is being used and delete data that is redundant.

- Implement Master Data Management - again, much easier said than done.

Example 3: Multitudinous Feeds

Question
Are there are many feeds?

Reason for question and why is this important?
Complex feeds with complex transformations are risky from a data point of view. Many feeds are "black boxes", and often no-one knows what they do, they are generally poorly documented, and often have no owner.

Anecdote

In once organisation I worked in there were 7,000 (yes, seven thousand) data feeds into *one* department.

Complex feeds will often transform data from a source state to a target state. The transformation may be incorrect. The transformation may have worked well at the time it was written. Now? Who knows?

Each transformation may auto-populate with default values, Many transformations may contain hard coded numbers, feeds may drop data they don't like. The feed may rely on lookups to tables of, for example, current products, which may or may not be updated or even exist. In all cases, the problem is that the data is being modified, added to or deleted and no-one really knows how or why – it is a hidden activity.

A key principle of data architecture is that data lineage is transparent. This kind of architecture is anything but transparent.

What can be done?
- The "proper" solution is to analyse each feed and work out whether it is necessary. With large volumes it may actually be easier to either:
  - Create another feed that does the job of 10 others and then switch the others off.
  - Switch the others off anyway, and see who screams. This is somewhat a nuclear solution, but is very effective.

Example 4: Too Many Applications

Question
Do we have complex architecture with multiple applications doing the same job?

Reason for question and why is this important
Unfortunately many organisations have multiple applications doing the same job. There may be many reasons for this:

- Acquisitions, where the newly acquired organisation has a different applications stack.
- Multiple vendors selling into multiple divisions, and all being successful.
- Out of date applications that are being replaced at different rates

Multiple applications may have multiple data sources, multiple feeds, multiple data standards, and multiple data models. This increases complexity and complexity brings architectural risk.

What can be done?
The traditional solution is to buy a new application, and migrate all the data from the legacy systems into the new application (an exercise in itself). Of course, a more common occurrence is that the legacy systems are never actually removed, resulting in simply another application being added to the mix.

The best way to approach this is for the organisation to discover who is using systems and for what, and then migrating the data to something strategic. At this point beware of end user computing, as the users may then re-create the old system on someone's desktop machine.

Example 5: Siloed Business Process

Question
Are there are any siloed business processes?

Reason for question and why is this important
Each part of the organisation does the same thing, just very slightly differently. The difficulty here is that data may be collected and stored in different

ways, under different data models. It may then be very difficult to integrate. It may be difficult to achieve a global, organisation-wide view.

What can be done?
- Use of a common data model helps enormously.
- Alternatively it is possible to move towards a service-orientated business architecture, where one part of the organisation is a specialist in "customer on-boarding", another in "further advance lending", etc. This removes the "different process" problem.

Example 6: The Secret Data Factory

Question
Are there are any secret data factories?

Reason for question and why is this important?
This scenario exists when one part of the organisation invests a lot of time and money into solving their data problem. They may build a bespoke data warehouse, datamarts, even a data lake, populate it, create bespoke reporting and analytics, and as far as they are concerned have solved their data problem. The trouble is that no-one else knows about it.

From a data architecture view, there may be understandable resistance from the secret data factory to change anything that they have spent time and money creating. Equally, what they have designed may not work for the rest of the organisation. The result is a standoff - where the secret factory won't change, but the rest of the organisation can't move.

What can be done?
- Understand what the secret data factory has achieved and how it has done it.
- Analyse whether its approach would work in the wider organisation.
- Get the owners and creators on board so they can work together.

Example 7: Choke Points

Question
Are there are any choke points?

Reason for question and why is this important
Choke points are where demand for a business process has far exceeded the capacity of the business area to keep up. Architectural components are overloaded and frequently fail.

This will cause a number of data problems. First, within the part of the organisation under pressure, quality is likely to come a poor second to throughput, and second they are likely to attempt to find/create/invent a variety of totally ungoverned short-cuts to work around the problem. None of these will be overly concerned about data.

What can be done?
- Understand the impact of the choke point on data.
- If the risk is unacceptable then raise as an issue to the organisation.

Example 8: The New Acquisition

Question
Has the organisation ever expanded through acquisition?

Reason for question and why is this important
New acquisitions take time to integrate into the wider organisation. They will come with their own applications and data stores for everything from HR management to customer on-boarding. None of these will match those of the new parent. This pseudo-separation can last decades. It has been said that interfaces are where data most commonly goes wrong. Having this pseudo-separation will create many of these interfaces.

It is arguable that the most risky situation is the half-integrated old acquisition, where a series of tactical and half-baked solutions have tried to integrate the data, and never quite succeeded.

What can be done?
- Understand what is and is not integrated, and what can be integrated.
- Understand the differences between the new and old data, the architectures and how they are being amalgamated.
- Design transition states and a target architecture.

Example 9: The "Cool" Division

Question
Is one area of the organisation growing fast, or being seen as "the future" for the organisation?

Reason for question and why is this important
A rapidly growing part of the business, or one that is seen as a shining star, may well consider that it can ignore the processes, procedures or controls for data architecture. Alternatively will be growing so fast that there is no time to do things "properly."

These situations can create almost every architectural problem. Tactical solutions, siloed data constructs, secret data factories. All are likely.

The problem is it is much easier to do things right first time - especially in architecture - than to sort them out later. The "cool" division can be a factory creating expensive problems for the future. When the regulator comes along later and asks "so, can you prove to us you know where your data comes from?" then the organisation may be facing a hefty fine if the answer is "no." Equally if the management are not getting the information they need, or that information is wrong, then its unlikely they will be impressed.

What can be done?
- The organisation needs to understand what is being done and why, and what has been created.
- Some long and hard conversations may have to be made with the new division and they may need to devote additional resources to coming into line.

Example 10: The Half-finished Project

Question
Have there been any projects that have closed whilst only half-completed?

Reason for question and why is this important
A half-finished project will likely leave many loose ends which are then tied up in a haphazard and uncontrolled fashion. There are likely to be a lot of tactical fixes, potentially manual work-arounds, and whilst the "core" architecture may be good, last minute changes may compromise integrity of the data flow.

In a delivery project, core functionality may be implemented first, and controls and testing completed towards the end. Projects that are not completed often leave untested and poor quality data in the organisation's information systems environment. These may be feeding poor quality data into the organisations systems, or corrupting good data already in place.

What can be done?
- Make a list of the loose ends and the solutions that have been used to complete them.
- Determine how they will create risks against data and the work needed to rectify.

Example 11: The Shiny Kit

Question
Has the organisation recently bought or installed any new elements into its information landscape?

Reason for question and why is this important
An organisation may spend a large amount on an application, and then will try and make the most of the expenditure by using the new purchase for purposes for which it is not explicitly designed. The use of any application for a purpose for which it is not necessarily designed risks the information that is being processed.

So, for example, an application may be being used as a data aggregator when it is really not designed for that purpose, or, worse, will corrupt or change data in transit. What comes out the end may not be fit for purpose, and because of the black box nature of the product, the consumer may not actually know.

What can be done?
- Understand the capabilities and limitations of the shiny new kit.
- If its use poses unacceptable risk to information, stop using it.

Example 12: The Tactical Solution

Question
Has the organisation implemented any short term tactical solutions in order to meet short term needs that are intended to be updated later?

Reason for question and why is it important
Most organisations are full of short term solutions. An issue is identified and a tactical solution is put in place as a sticking plaster to hold the information flow together until a better solution is found. In the normal course of events they will never actually be replaced.

Solutions that are implemented quickly, with limited – if any – testing, outside the normal governance process are often causes of major information risk.

What can be done?
- Understand the capabilities and limitations of the tactical solution.
- Understand its original purpose and what can be done to reduce risks.
- If risks are unacceptable then the organisation should look to modify or replace the solution.

Example 13: No Reference Architecture

Question
Has the organisation reference architecture standards so that different divisions or jurisdictions are constrained to create architectures in the same way?

Reason for question and why is this important?
Complexity breeds poor quality and architectural risk. With different countries all using different applications or data connected in different ways there is no consistency or, for that matter, economies of scale.

With no reference architecture it is very difficult to create consistent architectures that create good quality aggregate information. As a result architectures are likely to be different in each jurisdiction. Aggregate information may be incorrect, or nominally identical information in different markets may actually represent different things.

This can not only affect data, but can massively increase run costs for the organisation. A reference architecture stack, aligned to a global reference architecture, is key to bringing economies of scale and consistency and cost reduction across the organisation.

What can be done?
- Understand the effect of differing architectures on the data.
- Focus on the elements that cause the data pain and try and make all jurisdictions perform at least that element in the same way.

Example 14: End User Computing out of Control.

Question
How bad is the end user computing problem?

Reason for question and why is this important?
IT controlled systems are not the whole of the information landscape. Often, the majority of data manipulation occurs within business units, often in desktop productivity tools such as Microsoft Excel. It is common for this to get out of hand.

Anecdote:

One organisation I worked with had a month end process using 400,000 linked Excel Files.

The risk to information flow is massive. Most spreadsheets may contain errors. Hundreds or thousands of spreadsheets **will definitely** contain errors. Reports the business relies on for its operations should be created by controlled systems, not a member of the business team on their desktop.

What can be done?
- Understand the size of the problem.

- Understand to what extent end user computing duplicates work that can be done automatically.
- Look to bring end user computing under control, and create reports automatically.

Summary

The above examples may be familiar to anyone who has worked in large organisations. In many cases remediation will not be cost-effective. Generally the mess can be created far quicker than cleaning it up. This is especially true for data architecture.

However there are a number of potential allies. Industry regulators are not keen on poor data architectures as they lead to increased costs, greater risk, poor quality and hence to many issues for the organisation, not least customer dissatisfaction.

External and Internal Auditors are also allies. Data Governance is becoming more and more important in the assessment of the organisation, and poor data architecture may be brought up as a report point. Normally these are taken very seriously, so with an audit point behind you, theres a chance for rectification.

Then there is the law. There are a number of laws around data governance, data privacy and data accuracy, and if you can demonstrate that the organisation is in breach of the law, then there's a good incentive for solving the problem.

The last – but unfortunately often the weakest argument – is that the business are constrained from delivering what they need because of poor architecture.

Chapter 22: Designing Architectural Change

Introduction

After identification of pain points, the next stage is what to do about them. Although this may appear a slight recap of the previous chapter, in reality many solutions can apply to a single problem.

There is not a one-to-one mapping between problems described in the earlier chapter and solutions described here. Every organisation is different, and solutions that would work well in one organisation may make matters worse in another.

Every Data Architect should approach any problem with a wide range of possible solutions. These potential solutions can be offered up to see whether they would work in practice. The number of architectural solutions is essentially infinite, so in this chapter I have looked to start the reader on a journey to developing their own library of potential architectural solutions.

As said. No one pattern or solution is better than any other. They are all potentially good solutions, it depends what the problem is.

Centralisation

We will start with centralisation. Most readers will have seen the scenario where departments basically doing the same thing are collapsed into a single central unit, generally for the purpose of cost saving.

Typically this situation can arise with new departments selling different products, or to a different market. It is quicker and often easier to set up a parallel organisation with specialists for that customer type or market than to retrain existing employees or to increase capacity of existing systems. Existing systems may not be able to process for the new market or customer type, for example. However over time, as the new division is a success, the company realises that both parts are essentially doing the same thing and significant cost saves - and capacity increase - can result from amalgamating the two.

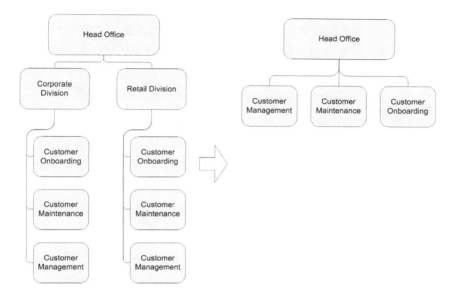

From a data architecture point of view, the advantage of centralisation is that one set of processes, centrally controlled, are less risky than disparate processes geographically dispersed. It is the "it's easier to look after if it is all in one place" view.

Federalisation

Federalisation is the opposite, and may occur when centralisation has failed, or where it is recognised that individual departments, countries, or business lines have more that differs than is common. It may then be more efficient to create separate solutions than to combine all solutions into one unit.

From a data architecture point of view, federalisation is most beneficial where differences are so pronounced that trying to fit all departments into one data model or process involves so many workarounds that the processes (or data) may as well be separate in the first place.

An example may be where an organisation has started selling to retail customers as well as direct to trade. If this is very successful, it may be easier to split the processes, as retail customers may need capabilities - such as call centres open late into the evening - that trade customers don't use.

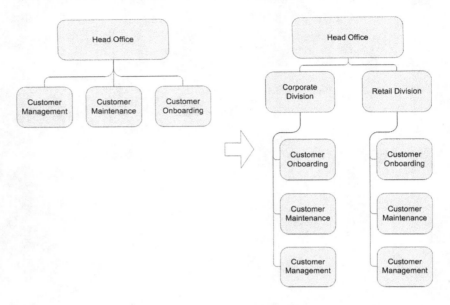

In general, splitting data up is much less of a problem than amalgamating it, so federalisation is much easier than centralisation. Key concerns would be ensuring the two divisions don't "drift" in their data and architectures to the point where the inevitable central reporting becomes difficult to achieve. Making sure there is a strong reference architecture will be a key role for the Enterprise Data Architect.

Supplementation

Another extremely common architectural change is where existing data is left as-is and a new process or data is piped into it. This may be the new department, the new acquisition, or the new product.

It can be easily seen that this is the first step into a siloed organisation, and as further elements are "supplemented" the problem will inevitably get out of hand.

However supplementation is easy and quick, and this often wins over "right." From a data architectural risk point of view, the big risk is the place where the two data flows meet. Does the "new" process have the same view of "customer" as the old? Does it have the same view of "customer balance?" Extreme care needs to be taken whilst amalgamating data from two different sources.

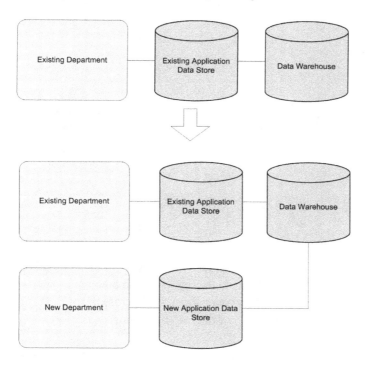

In short, I have included this not as a ideal solution, but in the full awareness that this is a common situation that will be encountered, and needs to be treated with care.

Reversing the Pipes

Reversing the pipes is an interesting architectural solution which involves using existing components, but reversing the data flow.

Consider the scenario below. Data is collected in individual country front end processing. It flows to individual country data stores, which then feed a central, "group" data store and group reporting.

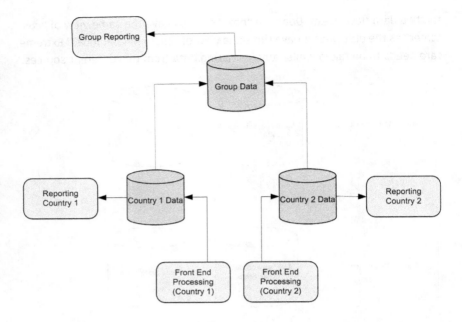

However, the organisation wants to migrate from many separate areas collecting data individually to a central data collection area. The problem the organisation may encounter is a lot of data connections exist across the organisation which will have to be replaced, and rewiring can be expensive.

Reversing the pipes enables a set of transition states getting the organisation to the desired target state with minimum disruption.

In this solution the individual divisions start by being the data collection point, which then pass data downstream to a central aggregation point. The architectural change creates a new, central data collection point and feeds data into the original aggregation point which then, rather than a copy of the local systems, is now the master. Data is then copied downstream to the local collection databases, which used to be the master copies and are now copies of the master.

Now, rather than customers ringing up country call centres who create the data which then feeds up to group reporting, the customer calls a global central call centre and then copies of the data are syndicated to the countries for in-country reporting.

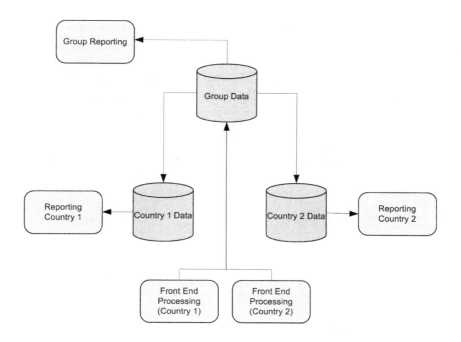

It is an interesting architectural solution which in theory brings a number of the benefits similar to centralisation, but without the drawbacks, as the countries still have their own "copy." However a problem still remains whether all of the individual country data fits into the global model. If not, then awkward workarounds will occur which may cause more problems than they solve.

This solution is particularly effective for introducing a new solution without disturbing the old. The new solution is implemented, and data is copied from the old solution to the new solution. The data origination initially remains in the old solution. Then at a cut-over point, the data flow is reversed, with the new system becoming the master.

Master Data Management (1)

Master Data Management (MDM) is an architectural change where, rather than each front end system or department maintaining their own copy of customer data, this data is held and maintained centrally.

From a data point of view, this means that each update to customer data (for example address changes) only has to be performed once, as the data is

shared across the organisation. It also has the advantage of central management, so quality can be enhanced in one place and the benefits shared by all.

The creation of a MDM solution, performed well, offers the possibility for a
step change in the ability of the organisation to process and use high quality
data.

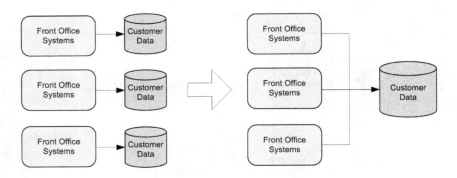

It is worth mentioning that as well as an *architectural* change the implementation of MDM is as much a *process* change, and in fact the changes to process
may be more difficult than the architectural ones.

In terms of architectural change this will involve reconfiguring all the of the
on-boarding systems to write to the same data store, and also reconfiguring
all of the downstream processes - which may include customer fufillment,
payments, billing and invoices, as well as potentially management reporting
and regulatory reporting - to read from the new data store.

So, whilst MDM implementation has a big upside to the organisation, it is not
an easy implementation, not least as the data store has to have appropriate
capability and structure for all the different areas of the organisation.

Master Data Management (2)

A second variety of MDM is where the organisation accepts that each department or division will have some data that is specific to them, and is not shared
with any other part of the organisation. However it also accepts that much
data – often customer and product data – is common.

This variety of MDM allows the individual division to keep their own data store for information specific to that division, but mandates the use of an enterprise-wide data store for the shared data.

This is a much easier implementation than the first variety of MDM described above, and may be a better solution for many organisations.

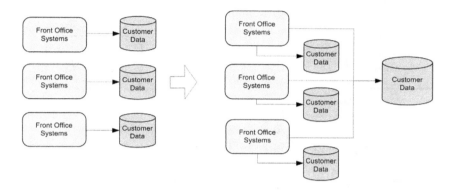

From a data architecture point of view, this form of MDM has some similarity with federalisation, in that it allows a scenario where the data that is difficult to fit into a 'one-size-fits-all' global MDM solution can be federated. It also allows the organisation to reap the benefits of centralised master data.

Simplification

A very common type of architectural change is simplification. The scenario shown in the diagram below is in no way uncommon, and as organisations have grown organically over time in some cases the data architecture becomes excessively complex, with links all over the organisation.

This is problematic for a number of reasons. There's the cost of maintenance, there is risk of failure, there are risks to data quality and there are impacts on the timeliness of the data, to name but a few. Generally, interfaces are where data pipelines go wrong, so reducing the number de-risks the data in the organisation.

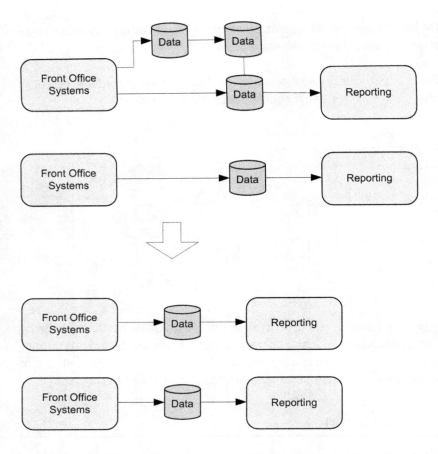

Simplifying the architecture makes everything better. It brings reduced risk, reduced run costs, better data lineage and transparancy. The challenge is implementation cost. Typically, all of the different databases have to be carefully unpicked to understand what happens to the data within them, how interfaces transform data, and this may be very difficult. A typical warehouse may have many hundreds - or thousands - of data feeds, so untangling the spaghetti to simplify it may take significant investment.

Data Model Changes

A fundamental base level architectural change is to change the data model. As described earlier in the book, the data model is the underlying structure of data within the organisation and supports its functionality. Unfortunately functionality changes over time, and when an original assumption might be that the organisation would not offer insurance products, later decisions may result in this view changing. Data relating to insurance products may have to be woven into the existing data model.

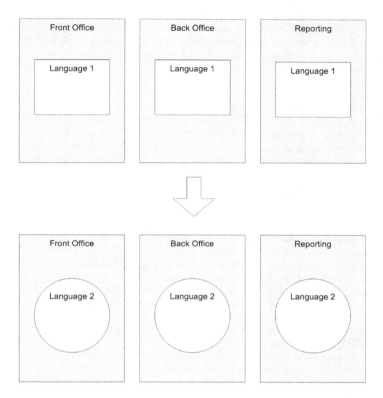

Another example is the concept of connected parties. If an organisation is looking to identify financial crime, then the concept of individuals who are not actually customers, but control customer accounts (examples like Power of Attorney) needs to be included within the overall data model.

Another typical reason is the purchase of a new core system, which works in a different way to the old. Changing the new system to match the old data model may not be possible or desirable, and it may be necessary to change the data model downstream to facilitate transfer of information.

The importance of data model changes cannot really be overestimated. The meaning of every element within the organisation may change, resulting in a change to every process, data transport, data warehouse and database. A change to the data model changes the data language of every report, extract, and application in the organisation.

Changes to the data model are risky. Extreme care needs to be undertaken to map one data model to the next. For some areas, months of careful analysis may be required to ensure the effective transfer of information and to ensure the information flows within the organisation are not broken.

Removing Blockers

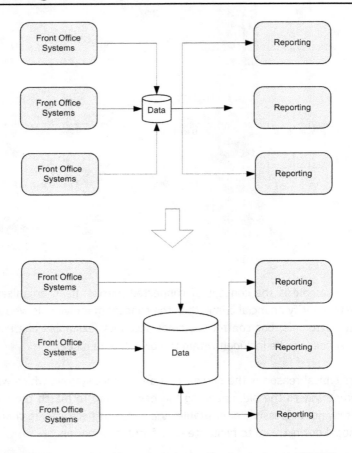

A very common type of architectural change is the removal of blockers. In an ideal world, data should flow seamlessly through the organisation. However this is not always the case. Many organisations have:

- Systems running at capacity and downstream consumers have to wait for data.
- Systems that provide data that requires significant rework.
- Systems that have a prioritised schedule and if you're at the bottom of the schedule you'll get data late or, worse, not at all.

These blockers have detrimental affects across the organisation. It is a natural consequence of blockers that parts of the organisation subject to the block will look to work around them. The result?

- Increased risk to the organisation - workarounds are often either informal and/or poorly governed.
- Shadow IT - parallel processes that exist in duplication of the approved pattern.
- Increased run costs.
- Poor data quality.

From an architecture point of view, an architectural change to remove a blocker decreases risk, increases throughput, and overall increases the opportunity for the organisation to get data right.

Globalisation

Globalisation is a very common scenario. At the start of the process the organisation may have several different divisions existing in each country. Each division does their own thing, with their own applications, data stores, data models, and reports to the individual country regulator.

When moving to a global model all of these differences need to be ironed out, so that at a group level all the countries operate in the same way, allowing results to be amalgamated for group reporting.

A further variation of this is the introduction of a mandatory global reference data architecture. Here organisations mandate the type and nature of data architecture for any division joining the group. This may result in major upheaval for the individual division as it has to remake all its systems to fall in line with the global model.

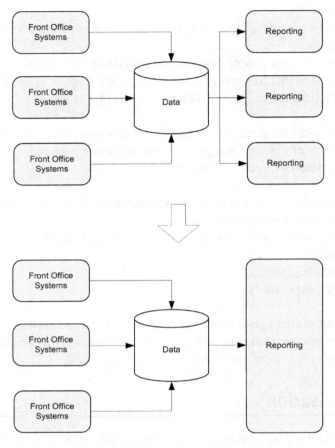

From a data point of view, globalisation often creates initial chaos, as it is found that all of the various reporting systems in each country speak different (data) languages. However, after this has been addressed, the overall effect to the organisation is positive.

Capability and Redundancy

One of the problems an organisation can face is the issue of redundancy and resilience. This can easily occur if multiple siloed data pipelines are developed, each independent of each other, and each without a failover mode.

There are various ways that the resilience of the organisation can be improved, and one of these is to increase the linkage between systems, so that one system can do the job of another if there is a failure.

In the example above, data is copied to multiple databases and the reporting software can read from any. The failure of any one of the pipelines is therefore protected.

The way this is implemented is that the database itself is multipally repli-cated, with fail-over between each copy. The ingest pipeline isn't generally replicated, but any failure would be attempted again and again until it worked, with the database well aware of the last successful update. At the point where the ingest pipeline was successful (for example when the replica database was up and running) the all records from the point of failure would update at once.

This in itself can cause failure, as too many record updates at one time can overload the database. Therefore being aware of cascading failures as systems are coming online is important.

Timing

I covered the various types of data in motion in a previous chapter. A key change an organisation can make is to move from a legacy batch process to a more modern API or streaming architecture.

As everything is now on the move, care must be taken in respect of data integrity. Extreme care needs to be taken that data arrives in the same state as transmitted, and that messages are controlled in respect of data quality.

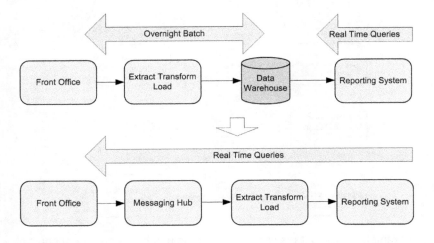

Unification

Unification occurs when there are a number of processes all using different approaches and/or different applications. The movement onto one application unifies the data, reduces complexity, and creates a common platform for reporting.

The cause of such an architecture is often expansion over time, as the organisation has bought new systems and expanded its product range. The old system may not have coped with a new product, so a new system was purchased.

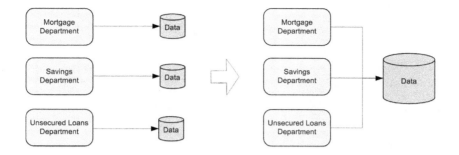

Customers of the new product were held in the new system, customers of the old product in the old system. It was certainly the easiest solution at the times, especially when it was not known whether the new product would be a success, but over time this brings architectural fragility, a poor view of the customer and barriers to change.

This change also increases staff mobility, as the applications used across the organisation are now the same, so it is possible for staff to move to branch from the contact centre, or to the savings department from the mortgage department. This change also reduces overall training costs as there is only one system to be trained on.

I would add that from a data point of view this architectural change is generally positive, as it unifies the data in one place, and in one model, and in a model which is inter-operable between departments. As such it enables a holistic view of the organisation across all data sets. This is generally a good excuse to clean up the data quality and purge decades-old (and incorrect) customer details.

Collapse of the Clones

The final example of architectural changes is where there are many departments, all doing more or less the same thing in the same way. Each is a clone of the others. This may occur when an organisation buys a competitor, and apart from some rebranding, leaves the competitor systems and processes in place. You therefore end up with multiple, identical pipelines. Collapsing the clones places all the information together and also reduces the number of applications.

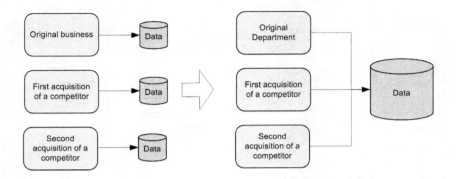

From an architecture point of view, this kind of change is generally positive, as it means that all data is now in the same language and the same place, allowing for much more effective management.

However this kind of change can be very difficult if the data model of the various clones is different.

The name I use for this architectural change, incidentally, comes from a real project where exactly this happened. The organisation bought multiple competitors, and ended up with many identical pipelines. The project to bring all of the clones into line and merge them into one system was called "Collapse of The Clones."

Summary

The above examples are in no way a comprehensive list of the way in which architecture can change. Every organisation is different and will face different problems. However it should give a feel for the potential changes that may be necessary and the reasons that they may occur.

It will be the role of the Enterprise Architect, and the Business Process, Data and Application architects, to design in detail a solution that addresses the root causes for each pain point in each individual organisation.

Chapter 23: Implementing Architectural Change

Introduction

So, having considered the pain points that may exist, examples of architectures and examples of architectural change, what needs to be done in a real life scenario in order to implement architectural change?

Architectural change is hard. Fundamentally architectural remediation requires a rethink of the way the organisation fits together. Data architecture is likely to have a knock-on effect on the business, technology and application architectures. However, it is still better to rectify "The Wrong Architecture" than to try and solve an unsolvable problem.

A classic example is multiple sources of data in the organisation. There is no point remediating dozens of sets of customer data individually. Not only will this take excessive time, but by comparing data sets a full, good data set may emerge. Alternatively, it may be necessary to think about implementing a "golden source" (Master Data Management) solution, where the disparate data stores are replaced by one source to which all the others refer.

However if architectural changes is required, then what considerations are needed, and what frameworks exist to help the organisation navigate such changes effectively?

This chapter looks to cover this ground.

Approaching Architectural Change

Alignment with Enterprise Architecture

Any architectural change needs to be aligned with the overall enterprise architecture. In many organisations there will already be a roadmap for the future state architecture, and many issues within data architecture may have already been identified and the most appropriate solution determined, and potentially documented and agreed. Alternatively, changes in business architecture - for example divestment of a division - may significantly affect the viability or need for changes to data architecture.

Even in the event the data architecture changes are not covered by pre-existing planned change, changes will need to be agreed with the architectural function. If there are deviations from the long term architectural direction, and especially if there are changes that make the achievement of the long term architectural vision more difficult, this needs to be thoroughly discussed, and reasons for deviation understood.

Validation of Solution

Before any architectural change occurs, the solution needs to be validated. A detailed assessment must be made of the as-is state, and how the movement to the target state will occur and how it will positively impact the organisation. This validation should cover all the elements of architecture affected.

This detailed assessment is vital. It is perfectly possible for a solution to look very plausible from a high level, but only when being planned in detail does information appear that will change the effort involved. Any implementation project needs to ensure that the high level view is supported by the low level facts.

Define Objectives

The implementation needs to clearly define its objectives. What is it trying to achieve? How will it be achieved? Importantly, how will it be measured? An example of an objective may be:

To replace the current 100 feeds into the finance department with 5 feeds, within six months from project start. This is in order to simplify the current complex manual integration required within the finance department and reduce the number of days required for the integration process from the current 10 to 2, and with significantly better quality output.

This objective clearly states what will occur, why it is occurring, and how it will be measured (number of feeds, and the reduction in number of days of effort from the finance department).

Transition States

However it may not be possible to move directly from one architectural state to another. It may be necessary to design and implement transition states that the architecture will pass through on the way to the final design.

Transition states are intermediate states that facilitate the transposition of the organisation from one architectural state to another. Performing architectural change in this manner is less risky than making a "big bang" change from one state to the next. The analogy of architectural change is being akin to moving the rooms of a house around, and the foundations of the new extension have to be put in place before work can continue to build new rooms. There will be a number of sequences that could occur, and the selection of the optimal sequence is the not-inconsiderable task of the Enterprise Data Architect.

An example may be MDM transition states. The initial state is separate data stores. The next stage is one department migrates its customer data onto the MDM solution, and retains its own data store for specialist data. Then the next department does the same, and finally the third.

Another example is the replacement of individual accounts departments in many sites with one central accounts department. First one site is migrated in, then the next, until all have been consolidated. The architectural implementation not only has to consider the start and end states, but also all the intermediate states. What will occur, for example, when half the sites have migrated? What will the organisation look like? How will processes work?

Governance

For each element of architectural change there needs to be governance. The change methodology needs to control the overall change in order to ensure that it is delivered as anticipated, and materialises the expected benefits, and is in line with the organisation's risk appetite. The governance will include, but not be limited to:

- Auditing the overall design and transition states against the overall organisational principles. These may include data principles, security principles, and risk and compliance principles.

- Ensuring the proposed changes support the organisational attitude to risk, and/or that transition states are managed to minimise risk to the organisation.

- Ensure that business continuity is considered in each area of change. What will occur if there is a disaster during the change process, how will the business recover? Typically business continuity is established after a steady state is achieved. Not only does the organisation need to ensure that at each transition point a business continuity plan exists, but that it is continuously updated as the change progresses.

- Ensuring an appropriate review or quality assurance mechanism is in place for the project.

- Ensuring a transparent link between the requirements of the overall project and what is being delivered. It is surprisingly easy for the original requirements to get lost as solutions are developed, and continuously refined, until a point is reached where the solution is technically mature, but shifts in functionality over time have meant that the original aim is no longer achieved.

- Ensuring that roll-back procedures are in place in case the change does not deliver the promised benefits, or (worse) actually creates problems more severe than those originally identified.

- An important stage is monitoring. The execution of the architectural change starts with as-is, and moves to each of the transition states in turn. The change is validated at each step, and the progress towards the overall goal monitored.

- What are the impacted areas? An important consideration is the identification of the impacted areas within the organisation. Architectural change is often upheaval. It is absolutely necessary to ensure that the parts of the organisation impacted are fully on board with proposed changes, and are prepared to support the project. The change needs to be explained to those areas. Equally the process needs to cover which individuals are impacted. The architectural change will need to answer questions such as:
  - How will job roles change?

- How will processes change?
- What effort is required from the business/IT areas?
- What information is needed from the business/IT areas?
- Who are the key stakeholders?
- Will applications change – if so, what departments use those applications?
- What infrastructure will change?

Impact on Business Operations

The change needs to be feasible from a business operation point of view, and this includes all the transition states. There is little point designing a transition state that will result in the organisation having to cease operations for any period of time. Realistically, a weekend is likely to be the maximum time it will be feasible for information systems to be "down."

It may be necessary, for example, to design the architectural change so there is a degree of parallel running, with business operations operating in both old and new architectural states for a period, and sharing the load between them until the new operation is proven.

Define Success Factors

It is necessary for the project to define the success factors for the architectural change. What needs to be in place for the operation to be a success?

One of the most important areas to consider when implementing architectural change across the organisation is how to prove the overall benefit of the change to the organisation, and how to prove that the change has been a success. The success of the change and the benefit it delivers need to be measurable.

Other Areas of Change

The reason that the organisation is undertaking architectural change is to improve. Depending on the nature of the architectural change it may well affect other areas. If the architectural change affects business processes, then the process analysts and process designers will of necessity been involved from the inception. Process architects and business architects need to ensure that they understand the nature of the changes and are involved at every step.

For example, if merging of data silos is performed to improve the ability of the organisation to remediate data, save costs, etc, the effect on upstream processes needs to be taken into account. If there is now only one downstream database, how will the multitude of upstream processes feed into it, and how will the data integrity and quality of those processes be maintained?

Dependencies

Allied to the concept of transition states, there may be dependencies between different elements of the solution, and as a result there may be a natural pattern to the overall change. For example, it will not be possible to run management information from the new database until it holds data. Therefore there is a natural dependency from management information to database population.

Planning

Lastly is planning and executing the change. It is likely that architectural change may be of a scale that functional change management needs to be set up. Equally, however, if the change is merely the deletion of feeds then this is less necessary.

Architectural Change Frameworks

To change from one architecture to another you need a framework. Several frameworks exist for architectural change. In the case of this book, I will refer to the TOGAF® framework, which at the time of writing had reached version 9.1.

The TOGAF® framework grew out of the US military architectural framework, but since 1995 has been adopted, modified, enhanced and published by The Open Group®. The Open Group® is a consortium of organisations with an interest in architectural change and an interest in pushing forward the disciplines of architecture, enterprise architecture and managed architectural change. The (9.1) version of the TOGAF® Architecture Development Method is shown in the diagram [reproduced with permission from The Open Group®].

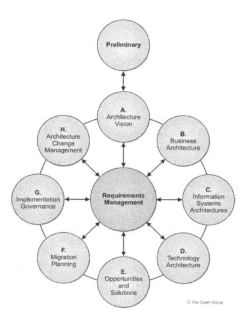

© The Open Group

The TOGAF® framework sets out a change methodology for architecture. It shows how an architectural vision for the organisation moves through to discovery and analysis work, and plans how to get to the vision from current state and the implementation of the solution.

For the purpose of this chapter we do not need to repeat the 600+ pages of the TOGAF® manual. However, I will step through the TOGAF® framework in my own words to give an idea of how architectural change can be approached.

Requirements
Requirements management is just that, and is the section of the TOGAF® framework that will manage the architecture requirements of the organisation. It should be noted here that this phase looks to perform a number of tasks. The organisation will identify requirements and the requirements management phase will look to ensure that these requirements are available for every element of the architecture development method throughout the project.

Preliminary Phase: Framework and Principles
The preliminary phase covers the elements that relate to the set-up of the overall method. This includes the way in which the organisation performs architec-

ture, and sets architectural standards and principles, and also the framework used. The preliminary phase will also start defining the requirements for the overall architecture and the business drivers as to why architectural change is necessary. This preliminary phase is about defining "where, what, why, who, and how we do architecture" in the enterprise concerned.

A: Architecture Vision

The architectural vision phase is similar to that of the corporate vision, described much earlier in this book. It is the development of the high level "where are we going" statement, and defines what will be delivered as part of the overall architectural development methodology. It also will look to develop a statement of architecture work that will be used to govern the project to implement the new architecture in the organisation.

B: Business Architecture

The business architecture element takes the architecture vision, and looks to develop a business architecture that will support the vision and will deliver on the business goals. Note that the business architecture is the way the business fits together, and is the first part of the four elements that take the organisation's vision and translate it into a target state. In architecture, as in data, business leads the way. This phase will assess the current business architecture, note issues and gaps, and design a future target state that will address them.

C: Information Systems Architecture

Information systems architecture is split into two elements, data and application. This phase takes the overall architecture vision, and the business architecture developed in the previous phase, and uses this to determine a data and application architecture that will support both. In the same way as the previous phase, this phase will assess the current data and application architecture, note issues and gaps, and design a future target state that will address them.

D: Technology Architecture

In the same way, the next stage of the architectural development methodology looks at the technology architecture. This is the nuts and bolts – or in this case servers and networks – that will support the overall architecture. It takes its lead from the business, data and application architecture and looks to create a technology architecture that will support them. In the same way as the previous phase, this phase will assess the current technology architecture, note issues and gaps, and design a future target state that will address them.

E Opportunities and Solutions
This phase is an aggregation phase. All the various roadmaps and design architectures are taken together and a complete framework for the target architecture is developed, incorporating all elements. This phase will also look at approaches to the overall implementation of the target architecture, as to whether it is necessary to create intermediate steps between the current architecture and the defined future architecture that will support the business vision.

F: Migration Planning
After determining the future vision, the next step is to define how the organisation will get there. The migration planning phase will finalise both the target end state architecture and also the way in which it will be achieved. This will include intermediate architectural steps (if necessary) and how transitions will work from one step to another.

This phase will also look to identify how the architectural change will fit in with the rest of the organisation. This will include how it will interact with the business and IT elements being changed and also how it will interact with the organisation's change function.

G: Implementation Governance
The objective of the next phase is to ensure that the implementation of the target architecture is performed correctly. This phase will be looking to ensure that the delivered architecture meets business needs, is what was required, and delivers what was promised.

H: Architecture Change Management
The final phase of the architectural development methodology is the phase that keeps the architectural development in line in the future, and that the overall governance framework is put into place.

Other architectural change frameworks apart from TOGAF exist. In fact, TOGAF was not even the first, though it is arguably the most popular. Wikipedia currently lists 38 different frameworks, and also notes that this is not a comprehensive list.

Example of Architectural Change

The above section is a little dry, so I will try and make the architectural change a little more real by walking through an example. I will again use the example of siloed data. Let us assume that we have five silos of customer data.

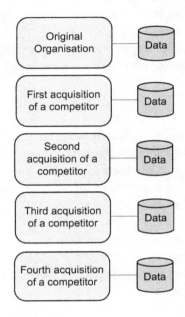

This may be because the organisation has five product categories (say, mortgages, savings, loans, insurance, current accounts), or may have bought/absorbed four other organisations and hence ended up with five sets of customer data, some of which may or may not overlap. The actual effort of merging these five silos is complex in the extreme, but I will look at this from a high level, and from the point of architecture only.

- A preliminary stage would be necessary that sets out the framework to be employed – for example a decision to employ the TOGAF® Framework ADM.

- Phase A is Vision. From a methodology perspective, the most important task at this point is to decide what the organisation wants. Is one set of customer data appropriate? There might be a wish to retain separate data systems if there was a strategic intention to sell off one of the silos. In this case, I have assumed that the intention is to amalgamate them all, in which case the target state is one (admittedly large) silo.

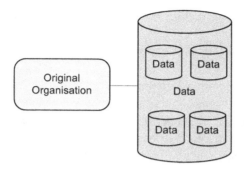

- The Requirements phase would pick up and manage the requirements for the overall project – this may be business, data, application or technology requirements.

- Phase B - Business Architecture - will examine how business processes can be amalgamated, how the organisation will work with only one silo, what will have to change and how the business moves from one state to another.

- Phase C - Information Systems Architecture - will take the work already accomplished and move onto the amalgamation of data stores. This will be a daunting task, and transition states will be critical. Will the business merge all data at once – 5 to 1 in a "big bang" approach, or will it amalgamate two silos first as a pilot (possibly the largest and smallest, or the two smallest, whichever works better) and then add in a silo at a time? Data that flows into and out from the existing silos will have to be re-routed.

  Should the data be moved, then de-duplicated (as in the diagram above), or is it better to de-duplicate, then move? The same will apply to applications. There may be a set of applications per silo, and they may – or may not – be compatible. There will have to be a decision to turn one off, migrate data, and do this in a controlled manner.

- Phase D - Technology Architecture - will look from the technology perspective. Currently there may be five servers, five back-up sites, five sets of network infrastructure. These will have to be amalgamated and this stage will determine how this will occur.

- Phase E - Opportunities and Solutions - then brings this all together. This phase will set out a roadmap for the overall architectural change, and also the combined end state vision.

- Phase F - Migration Planning - takes the output and will plan how to deliver the change. In this particular case it will involve the whole business as the information flows throughout the business will be fundamentally reorganised. It may be possible, with careful design, for one silo (the biggest) to remain unchanged, if everything else is merged into it, and for the impact on the overall organisation to be minimised.

- Phase G - Implementation Governance - is actually about governing the change. The project may be in full flow, with many moving parts. Phase G will look to ensure that the implementation is put in place according to the roadmap and plan.

- Phase H - Change Management - will finally ensure that an architecture governance framework is in place, to try and ensure that the situation never occurs again.

Summary

Within this chapter I have examined architectural change in more detail. I have discussed the considerations that may drive architecture change, and the way they can be approached.

I have introduced the reader to the TOGAF® Architectural Development Methodology, stepped through this at a high level and then given a practical example of how this can be applied to a real-life problem of siloed data.

Chapter 24: Endnote

We have reached the end of the material in this book. Over these pages I have endeavoured to:

- Introduce the reader to data architecture, the types of Data Architect, the role and the day to day work that they do.
- Introduce the building blocks of data architecture, and cover those that are critical to the Data Architect in some detail.
- Bring the above together into data architecture principles, example architectures, pain points and architectural change.

I have assumed no initial knowledge, and have tried to cover both the basics and more intermediate knowledge that would normally only be gained through years of experience.

The above is, in my view, a good grounding in the discipline of data architecture. The aim of this book is, however, only to introduce the subject, it is only the beginning of the whole story. That whole story is being written every day in organisations across the world, as they create and populate data structures in their quest to find, for them, the perfect data flow.

For now though, I hope I have achieved my aim, and that the reader has finished this book more knowledgeable, and more interested, in data architecture. It is, for me, one of the most interesting areas of work today.

Exciting, isn't it?

John Parkinson
2023

APPENDICES

Appendix 1: Bibliography

Data Governance, John Ladley, Morgan Kaufman, 2012.

Data Governance Tools, Sunil Soares, MC Press, 2014.

Data Stewardship. David Plotkin, Morgan Kaufman, 2014.

Non-Invasive Data Governance, Robert Seiner, Technics Publications, 2014.

Performing Information Governance, Giordano, IBM Press, 2015.

Master Data Management and Data Governance, Berson & Dubov, McGraw Hill, 2011.

Selling Information Governance to the Business, Sunil Soares, MC Press, 2011.

The IBM Data Governance Unified Process, Soares, MC Press, 2011

COBIT 5, Information Systems and Control Association (ISACA), 2013.

Data Management Body of Knowledge, DAMA-BOK, Mosely et Al, Data Management Association, 2010.

Data Warehouse Design, Modern Principles and Methodologies, Golfarelli et al, 2009, McGraw-Hill

Data Integration Blueprint and Modeling, Giordano, IBM Press, 2011

The Corporate Information Factory, Inmon et al, Wiley, 1999

The Ultimate Guide to Business Process Management, Panagacos, 2012.

Business Process Change, Paul Harmon, Morgan Kaufman, 2007

Business Process Analysis, Geoffrey Darnton, Requirements Analytics, 2012

The Basics of Process Mapping, Robert Damelio, CRC Press, 2011

Practical Data Migration, Johny Morris, BCS Learning and Development, 2012

Knowledge Management Toolkit, Swiss Agency for Development and Co-operation, SDC, 2009.

Knowledge Management in Theory and Practice, Kimiz Dalkir, Elsvier, 2005.

Introduction to Knowledge Management, Filemon A Uriarte Jr, ASEAN Foundation, 2008.

Knowledge Management Strategy, World Health Organisation, 2005.

Knowledge Management Tools and Techniques Manual, Dr Ronald Yound, APO 2010.

Knowledge Management Tools and Techniques, Leask et Al, IDEA, 2008

Case Studies in Knowledge Management, Murray Jennex, IDEA 2005

The Knowledge Management Toolkit: Practical Techniques for Building a Knowledge Management System, Second Edition, Pearson Education 2002.

Learning to Fly, Collison and Parcell, Capstone 2004.

Managing Successful Projects with PRINCE 2, TSO 2009

Credit Risk Management, Gestel and Baesens, Oxford University Press, 2009.

Practitioner's Guide to Data Quality Improvement, David Loshin, Morgan Kaufman, 2011

Information Quality Applied, Larry English, Wiley, 2009

Improving Data Warehouse and Business Information Quality, Larry English, Wiley, 1999

Measuring Data Quality for Ongoing Improvement, Laura Sebastian-Coleman, Morgan Kaufman, 2013

Business Analysis, Third Edition, Paul, Cadle & Yeates, BCS, 2014

The Business Analysts' Handbook, Podeswa, Course Technology, 2009

Master Data Management in Practice, Cervo & Allen, Wiley, 2011

Master Data Management, David Loshin, Morgan Kaufman, 2009

The Multidimensional Manager, Connelly, McNeil and Mosiman, Cognos, 1999

Business Intelligence Strategy, Boyer et al, MC Press, 2010

The Performance Manager, Connelly, McNeil & Mosimann, Cognos, 2007

Blank Pages